A-LEVEL
STUDENT GUIDE

OCR

Physical Education

Physiological factors affecting performance

Sue Young

HODDER
EDUCATION
AN HACHETTE UK COMPANY

This Student Guide has been written specifically to support students preparing for the OCR A-level Physical Education examinations. The content has been neither approved nor endorsed by OCR and remains the sole responsibility of the author.

Hachette UK's policy is to use papers that are natural, renewable and recyclable products and made from wood grown in well-managed forests and other controlled sources. The logging and manufacturing processes are expected to conform to the environmental regulations of the country of origin.

Orders: please contact Bookpoint Ltd, 130 Park Drive, Milton Park, Abingdon, Oxon OX14 4SE. Telephone: (44) 01235 827827. Fax: (44) 01235 400401. Email: education@bookpoint.co.uk. Lines are open from 9 a.m. to 5 p.m., Monday to Saturday, with a 24-hour message answering service. You can also order through our website: www.hoddereducation.co.uk.

© Sue Young 2020

ISBN 978-1-5104-7208-2

First printed 2020

First published in 2020 by
Hodder Education,
An Hachette UK Company
Carmelite House
50 Victoria Embankment
London EC4Y 0DZ

www.hoddereducation.co.uk

Impression number 10 9 8 7 6 5 4 3 2 1

Year   2023 2022 2021 2020

Cover photo: ohishiftl/Adobe Stock

Typeset by Integra Software Services Pvt. Ltd, Pondicherry, India

Printed in Italy

A catalogue record for this title is available from the British Library.

Contents

Content Guidance

Questions & Answers

■ Getting the most from this book

Exam-style questions

Commentary on the questions

Tips on what you need to do to gain full marks.

Sample student answers

Practise the questions, then look at the student answers that follow.

Commentary on sample student answers

Read the comments showing how many marks each answer would be awarded in the exam and exactly where marks are gained or lost.

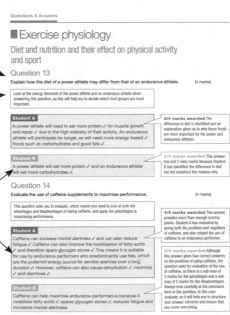

■About this book

This Student Guide covers the topics required for OCR A-level specification H555 Paper 1: Physiological factors affecting performance. Remember that this is a guide, not a textbook. It provides a summary of what you need to know and understand for your exam, but is intended to complement, not replace, your textbook and class notes.

The Content Guidance section follows the headings set out in the OCR specification. It is divided into three main topics:
- Applied anatomy and physiology
- Exercise physiology
- Biomechanics

Use the knowledge check questions as you progress through each topic to test your understanding, and take on board the exam tips in order to avoid falling into the traps that most commonly result in students losing marks. At the end of each topic area there is an overall summary of the content covered — if you are unable to offer a detailed explanation of any part of this, you should work through this section again to clear up any misunderstanding.

The Questions & Answers section begins by setting out the format of the exam papers, giving you advice and important tips on how to maximise your marks on the different elements of the paper. It also explains the levels system used for extended questions.

This is followed by a series of sample questions. After each of these questions there are some example answers from students illustrating both best practice as well as not such good practice. You should attempt all of these questions yourself and compare your answers with these while reading the detailed comments to help improve your understanding of what is required to achieve top marks.

Content Guidance

■ Applied anatomy and physiology

Skeletal and muscular systems

For this topic you need to be able to analyse movement in physical activities and sport, applying your knowledge of muscular contraction.

Structure and function of bones, joints and connective tissue

The skeleton is a framework connected together by joints (Figure 1). Joints are necessary for muscles to lever bones, thus creating movement. A joint is formed where any two or more bones meet, and is classified according to how much movement it allows. There are three types of joint: fibrous, cartilaginous and synovial. In your exam you will be analysing synovial joints, which have several common features, as shown in Table 1.

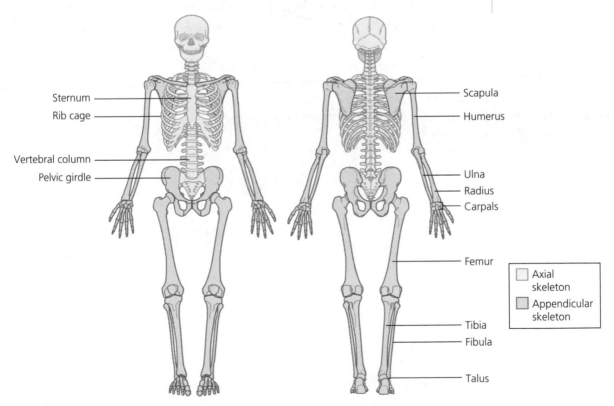

Figure 1 The bones of the axial and appendicular skeleton

Table 1 Structure and function of a synovial joint

Feature	Structure and function
Articular/hyaline cartilage	This covers the ends of the bones at a joint and is there to prevent friction between the articulating bones
Joint capsule	A tough fibrous layer of tissue encasing the joint, which is present to protect and strengthen the joint
Synovial membrane	The inner layer or lining to the joint capsule; it secretes synovial fluid
Synovial fluid	Fluid that fills the joint capsule, which nourishes the articular cartilage and prevents friction
Ligament	Strong, fibrous connective tissue that provides stability by joining bone to bone
Pads of fat	Areas of fat that act as shock absorbers in the joint
Bursa	A fluid-filled sac located between a tendon and a bone that is there to reduce friction

Exam tip

Table 2 gives you all the necessary information, so make sure you learn it but also that you can apply that knowledge to images of joint movement.

Joint movement and muscles

For your exam you need to know the information in Table 2 for all the joints listed.

Table 2 Joint movement analysis

Joint movement	Plane	Agonist muscles	Antagonist muscles
The **shoulder** is a **ball and socket** joint. The articulating bones are the **humerus** and the **scapula**.			
Flexion	Sagittal	Anterior deltoid	Latissimus dorsi
Extension	Sagittal	Latissimus dorsi	Anterior deltoid
Abduction	Frontal	Middle deltoid	Latissimus dorsi
Adduction	Frontal	Latissimus dorsi	Middle deltoid
Horizontal flexion	Transverse	Pectoralis major	Latissimus dorsi
Horizontal extension	Transverse	Latissimus dorsi	Pectoralis major
Medial rotation	Transverse	Teres major	Teres minor
Lateral rotation	Transverse	Teres minor	Teres major
Circumduction	Mix of all three	Mix of the above	Mix of the above
The **elbow** is a **hinge** joint. The articulating bones are the **humerus**, the **radius** and the **ulna**.			
Flexion	Sagittal	Biceps brachii	Triceps brachii
Extension	Sagittal	Triceps brachii	Biceps brachii
The **wrist** is a **condyloid** joint. The articulating bones are the **radius**, the **ulna** and the **carpals**.			
Flexion	Sagittal	Wrist flexor	Wrist extensor
Extension	Sagittal	Wrist extensor	Wrist flexor
The **hip** is a **ball and socket** joint. The articulating bones are the **pelvic girdle** and the **femur**.			
Flexion	Sagittal	Iliopsoas	Gluteus maximus
Extension	Sagittal	Gluteus maximus	Iliopsoas
Abduction	Frontal	Gluteus medius/minimus	Adductors (brevis magnus and brevis longus)
Adduction	Frontal	Adductors (brevis magnus and brevis longus)	Gluteus medius/minimus
Medial rotation	Transverse	Gluteus medius/minimus	Gluteus maximus
Lateral rotation	Transverse	Gluteus maximus	Gluteus medius/minimus

→

Table 2 Joint movement analysis (continued)

Joint movement	Plane	Agonist muscles	Antagonist muscles
The **knee** is a **hinge** joint. The articulating bones are the **femur** and the **tibia**.			
Flexion	Sagittal	Biceps femoris (hamstring group)	Rectus femoris (quadriceps group)
Extension	Sagittal	Rectus femoris (quadriceps group)	Biceps femoris (hamstring group)
The **ankle** is a **hinge** joint. The articulating bones are the **tibia**, the **fibula** and the **talus**.			
Plantar flexion	Sagittal	Gastrocnemius/soleus	Tibialis anterior
Dorsiflexion	Sagittal	Tibialis anterior	Gastrocnemius/soleus

Movement patterns associated with these joints are shown in Figures 2 and 3.

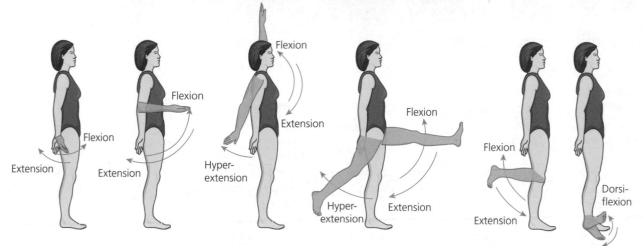

Figure 2 Movement patterns in the sagittal plane: (a) flexion and extension at the wrist, elbow, shoulder, hip and knee joints; (b) dorsiflexion and plantar flexion at the ankle joint

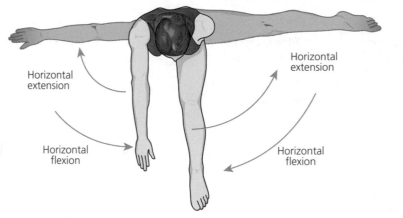

Figure 3 (a) Movement patterns in the transverse plane: horizontal extension and horizontal flexion

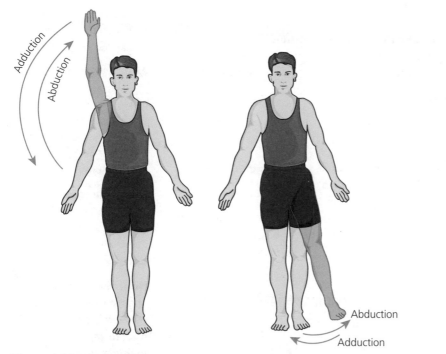

Figure 3 (b) Movement patterns in the frontal plane: abduction and adduction at the shoulder and hip joints

Knowledge check 1

Complete the blanks in the following movement analysis table:

Joint action	Plane	Agonist	Antagonist
Hip abduction			
		Rectus femoris	

Functional roles of muscles and types of contraction

Roles of muscles

An agonist is the muscle responsible for creating movement at a joint. The antagonist is the muscle that opposes the agonist. The fixator is a muscle that stabilises one part of a body while another part moves.

Types of contraction

An isotonic contraction is where the muscles are contracting and changing length.

There are two types of movement that take place as a result:
- Concentric contraction — when a muscle shortens under tension.
- Eccentric contraction — when a muscle lengthens under tension.

An isometric contraction is where the muscle is under tension, but there is no visible movement.

Exam tip

In an eccentric contraction the muscle is acting as a brake.

Analysis of movement

In movement analysis you need to be able to identify in the shoulder, elbow, wrist, hip, knee and ankle the joint type, movement produced, agonist and antagonist muscles involved in the movement, and type of muscle contraction taking place.

Skeletal muscle contraction

Structure and nervous stimulation of a motor unit

A **motor unit** consists of a **motor neurone** and its muscle fibres. A nerve impulse is conducted down the axon of the motor neurone by a nerve **action potential** to the **neuromuscular junction**. Here there is a small gap called the synaptic cleft. An action potential is unable to cross the synaptic cleft without a **neurotransmitter** called acetylcholine. In addition, the sequence of impulses has to be of sufficient intensity to create a muscle action potential resulting in all of the muscle fibres in a motor unit contracting, fulfilling the **all-or-none law**.

Muscle contraction during exercise of differing intensities and during recovery

Muscle fibre type and exercise intensity

Motor neurones stimulate one of three types of muscle fibre. Slow oxidative fibres (type I) are better adapted to low-intensity, long-duration exercise. They produce their energy aerobically and have specific characteristics that allow them to use oxygen more effectively. Fast-twitch fibres can generate a greater force of contraction and produce most of their energy anaerobically. Fast oxidative fibres (type IIa) are more resistant to fatigue and are used for events such as the 1500 m in athletics, where a longer burst of energy is needed. Fast glycolytic fibres (type IIb) fatigue quickly and are used for highly explosive events such as the 100 m in athletics or powerlifting. Table 3 highlights the characteristics and functions of the three fibre types.

Table 3 The structural characteristics and functions of the three muscle fibre types

Structural characteristic	Type I	Type IIa	Type IIb
Motor neurone size	Small	Large	Large
Mitochondrial density	High	Medium	Low
Myoglobin content	High	Medium	Low
Capillary density	High	Medium	Low
PC and glycogen store	Low	High	High
Function			
Contraction speed (milliseconds)	Slow (110)	Fast (50)	Fast (50)
Motor neurone conduction capacity	Slow	Fast	Fast
Force produced	Low	High	High
Fatigability	Low	Medium	High
Aerobic capacity	Very high	Medium	Low
Anaerobic capacity	Low	High	Very high
Myosin ATPase/glycolytic enzyme activity	Low	High	Very high

Motor unit The motor neurone and its fibres, stimulated by its axon.

Action potential The positive electrical charge inside the nerve and muscle cells that conducts the nerve impulse down the motor neurone into the muscle fibres.

Neuromuscular junction Where the motor neurone and the muscle fibres stimulated by its axon meet.

Neurotransmitter A chemical that is released by neurones to transmit a nerve impulse across the synaptic cleft to the muscle fibre, e.g. acetylcholine.

All-or-none law Determines whether a stimulus is above the threshold required for the fibres in a motor unit to contract. If it is below this threshold, then none of them will contract.

Exam tip

Slow-twitch fibres are aerobic and fast-twitch fibres are anaerobic.

Exam tip

Make sure you know which type of fibre is linked to which sporting activity.

Knowledge check 2

Which type of muscle fibre is linked to endurance?

Muscle fibre type and recovery

Slow oxidative muscle fibres recover quickly, and it is possible to recruit them in approximately 90 seconds. To maximise their use in aerobic training the work-to-relief ratio needs to be low, at 1 : 1 or 1 : 0.5. Muscle fibre damage is not associated with aerobic activity because muscle contraction is not as explosive, so training can be performed more safely and frequently. The use of slow oxidative muscle fibres often takes place between heavy weight training sessions to increase blood flow and facilitate the healing process.

Fast glycolytic muscle fibres are more explosive and recruited for maximum intensity, which can result in **DOMS** due to eccentric muscle fibre damage. Therefore, fast glycolytic fibres will take longer to recover and, when used to exhaustion, recovery can take 4–10 days. After a maximal weight training session with a high work : relief ratio of 1 : 3, a minimum of 48 hours recovery should be taken before using the same muscle group again.

DOMS The delayed onset of muscle soreness felt 24–48 hours after exercise.

Summary

After studying this topic you should be able to:
- identify the joint type, movement produced, agonist and antagonist muscles involved and type of muscle contraction taking place, at the shoulder, elbow, wrist, hip, knee and ankle
- identify which plane of axis a joint movement takes place in
- explain the role of a muscle as an agonist, antagonist and fixator
- give the type of contraction as concentric, eccentric or isometric
- understand the structure and role of motor units in muscle contraction
- explain the following terms: motor unit, motor neurone, action potential, neurotransmitter and all-or-none law
- identify and explain the recruitment of the three different muscle fibre types during exercise of differing intensities and during recovery

Cardiovascular and respiratory systems

The heart at rest, during exercise and during recovery

Measuring stroke volume, heart rate and cardiac output assesses the efficiency of the heart.

Stroke volume

The volume of blood pumped out by the left ventricle in each contraction. On average, resting stroke volume (SV) is approximately 70 ml, but this value is much bigger in elite performers. Stroke volume increases as exercise intensity increases, but only up to 40–60% of maximum effort. Once a performer reaches this point, stroke volume plateaus because the ventricles do not have as much time to fill up with blood due to an increased heart rate.

Starling's law

increased venous return → greater diastolic filling of the heart → cardiac muscle stretched → more force of contraction → increased ejection fraction

Starling's law explains how stroke volume increases during exercise. This is when there is an increase in venous return, which leads to a greater diastolic filling, so the cardiac muscle is stretched. Consequently, a more powerful force of contraction takes place, which increases the **ejection fraction** and therefore increases stroke volume.

> **Ejection fraction** The percentage of blood pumped out by the left ventricle per beat.

Heart rate

Heart rate (HR) is the number of times the heart beats per minute. It increases with exercise — the higher the intensity, the higher heart rate (Figure 4). Maximum heart rate can be calculated as 220 minus the individual's age.

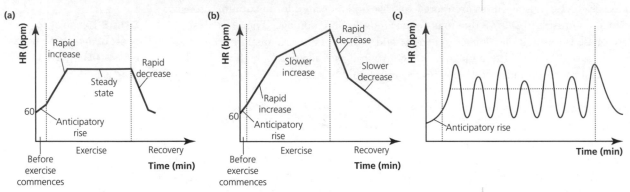

Figure 4 HR response to exercise of different intensities: (a) sub-maximal (aerobic), (b) maximal (anaerobic), (c) fluctuating intensities

A trained performer has a greater heart rate range because their resting heart rate is lower and maximum heart rate increases. Regular exercise causes hypertrophy of the heart, resulting in an increase in stroke volume and maximum cardiac output, and leading to bradycardia (a lower resting heart rate of below 60 beats per minute).

> **Knowledge check 3**
>
> How does maximum cardiac output differ for a trained performer? Explain the effect this has on performance.

Cardiac output

Cardiac output (Q) is the amount of blood pumped out by the left ventricle per minute:

$$Q = SV \times HR$$

Cardiac output stays the same at rest for both a trained and untrained performer. During exercise, maximum cardiac output increases due to an increase in HR and in SV. Cardiac output will increase as the intensity of exercise increases until maximum intensity is reached and then it plateaus. During exercise the increase in maximum cardiac output will have huge benefits for the trained performer as it will increase the oxygen carrying capacity of the blood to the working muscles.

> **Knowledge check 4**
>
> How does regular training affect cardiac output, stroke volume and heart rate?

Cardiac cycle

The cardiac cycle describes the process of the cardiac muscle contracting and the movement of blood through the heart chambers. Each complete cardiac cycle takes approximately 0.8 seconds. There are two phases: cardiac **diastole** is the relaxation of the cardiac muscle, and cardiac **systole** is the contraction of the cardiac muscle. The systolic and diastolic phases of the atria and ventricles are described in Tables 4 and 5.

> **Exam tip**
>
> Remember cardiac output is the same at rest for both a trained and untrained performer. It is maximum cardiac output that is higher in a trained performer.

Diastole The cardiac cycle phase involving relaxation of the cardiac muscle.

Systole The cardiac cycle phase involving contraction of the cardiac muscle.

Table 4 Atrial systole and diastole

Stage	Action of atria	Result
Atrial systole	Walls contract	Blood forced through the AV valves into the ventricles
Atrial diastole	Walls relax	Blood enters right atrium via the vena cava and the left atrium via the pulmonary vein but cannot pass into the ventricles as the AV valves are closed

Table 5 Ventricular systole and diastole

Stage	Action of ventricles	Result
Ventricular systole	Walls contract	Pressure of blood opens the semilunar valves and blood is ejected into the pulmonary artery to the lungs and aorta to the body; the AV valves shut
Ventricular diastole	Walls relax	Blood enters from atria via 'passive ventricular filling' — not due to atrial contraction; the semilunar valves are closed to prevent blood leaving the heart

Cardiac conduction system

The cardiac conduction system ensures that rate of the cardiac cycle increases during exercise to allow the working muscles to receive more oxygen. Heart muscle is myogenic because the beat starts in the heart muscle itself, with an electrical signal in the **sinoatrial node (SA node)**. From the SA node the electrical impulse spreads through the walls of the atria, causing them to contract (atrial systole). The impulse then passes through the **atrioventricular node (AV node)** where it is delayed for approximately 0.1 seconds to enable the atria to fully contract. The impulse then travels through the bundle of His, which branches into two bundles and into the Purkinje fibres, which in turn spread throughout the ventricles, causing them to contract (ventricular systole).

Regulation of heart rate during exercise

The rate at which impulses are fired from the SA node can be controlled by neural, hormonal and intrinsic factors.

Neural factors

These involve the sympathetic nervous system, which stimulates the heart to beat faster, and the parasympathetic system, which returns the heart to its resting level. These two systems are coordinated by the cardiac control centre (CCC) located in the **medulla oblongata** of the brain. The CCC is stimulated by chemoreceptors, baroreceptors and proprioceptors, and will then send an impulse through either the sympathetic system via the cardiac accelerator nerve to the SA node to increase heart rate or the parasympathetic system via the vagus nerve to the SA node to decrease heart rate:

- chemoreceptors → detect increase in blood carbon dioxide → CCC → sympathetic system → SA node increases heart rate

- baroreceptors → detect increase in stretch in the blood vessel walls → CCC → parasympathetic system → SA node decreases heart rate

- proprioceptors → detect increase in motor activity → CCC → sympathetic system → SA node increases heart rate

Sinoatrial node (SA node) A small mass of cardiac muscle found in the wall of the right atrium that generates the heartbeat. More commonly called the pacemaker.

Atrioventricular node (AV node) This slows the electrical current sent by the SA node before the signal passes down to the ventricles.

Knowledge check 5

How does the SA node control heart rate?

Exam tip

The sympathetic system speeds up heart rate for exercise and the parasympathetic system slows it down for recovery.

Medulla oblongata The most important part of the brain; it regulates processes that keep us alive.

Knowledge check 6

How does an increase in blood carbon dioxide affect heart rate?

Hormonal factors

Adrenaline is a stress hormone that is released by the sympathetic nerves and cardiac nerves during exercise. It stimulates the SA node, which results in an increase in both the speed and force of contraction, therefore increasing cardiac output.

Intrinsic factors

Changes in temperature will affect blood viscosity and the speed of nerve impulse transmission. In addition, venous return will increase, which stretches the cardiac muscle, stimulating the SA node, which in turn increases the force of ventricular contraction and therefore stroke volume.

Adrenaline A stress hormone that stimulates the SA node.

The vascular system at rest, during exercise and during recovery

The vascular system consists of a network of blood vessels that deliver oxygen and nutrients to the body tissues and take away waste products such as carbon dioxide.

Characteristics of blood vessels

- Veins have thinner muscle/elastic tissue layers, with blood at lower pressure, and they have valves and a wider lumen. Veins and venules have a thin layer of smooth muscle allowing them to venodilate and venoconstrict to maintain the flow of deoxygenated blood towards the heart.
- Arteries transport oxygenated blood to the muscles and have a higher pressure (with an elastic outer layer to cope with these fluctuations in pressure), a smaller lumen and a thick layer of smooth muscle. Arterioles also have a thick layer of smooth muscle, allowing them to vasodilate and vasoconstrict in order to regulate blood flow.
- Capillaries have characteristics that help gaseous exchange. Their walls are one cell thick, so there is a short diffusion pathway, and have a large surface area and a narrow diameter to slow blood flow down. Training increases capillary density.

Venous return mechanisms

During exercise, **venous return** increases. Active mechanisms are needed to help venous return:

- The skeletal muscle pump — when muscles contract and relax they press on nearby veins, causing a pumping effect and squeezing the blood back towards the heart.
- The respiratory pump — when muscles contract and relax during the inspiration and expiration process, pressure changes occur in the thoracic and abdominal cavities. These pressure changes compress the nearby veins and assist blood return back to the heart.
- Valves prevent the back-flow of blood.
- A thin layer of smooth muscle within the vein walls helps squeeze blood back towards the heart through venoconstriction.
- Gravity helps the blood return to the heart from the upper body.
- During recovery, low-intensity activity maintains the muscle and respiratory pumps to help return blood back to the heart.

Venous return The return of blood back to the right side of the heart via the vena cava.

Redistribution of cardiac output during exercise and recovery

During exercise it is important to redistribute blood to areas where it is most needed:

■ More blood needs to go to the muscles to increase the supply of oxygen and remove waste products such as a carbon dioxide and lactic acid.
■ More blood needs to go to the skin to regulate body temperature and get rid of heat through radiation, evaporation and sweating.
■ More blood needs to be directed to the heart because it is a muscle and requires extra oxygen during exercise.

Vascular shunt mechanism

The redistribution of blood flow is controlled by the vascular shunt mechanism. During exercise, **vasodilation** will occur in the arterioles supplying muscles to increase blood flow and therefore the supply of oxygen. **Vasoconstriction** will occur in the arterioles supplying non-essential organs such as the intestines and liver, decreasing blood flow.

Pre-capillary sphincters also aid blood redistribution. These are tiny rings of muscle located at the openings of capillaries. These relax around the muscles during exercise to increase blood flow and saturate the muscles with oxygen.

Vasomotor control

Both blood pressure and blood flow are controlled by the **vasomotor control centre (VCC)**, located in the medulla oblongata of the brain. During exercise, increases in carbon dioxide and lactic acid are detected by chemoreceptors and increases in the stretch of vessel walls are detected by baroreceptors. These receptors send impulses to the VCC, which redistributes blood flow through sympathetic stimulation. An increase in sympathetic stimulation causes vasoconstriction and a decrease in stimulation by the sympathetic nerves causes vasodilation.

Vasodilation Widening of the blood vessels to increase blood flow.

Vasoconstriction Narrowing of the blood vessels to reduce blood flow.

Vasomotor control centre (VCC) The control centre in the medulla oblongata that regulates blood flow and pressure.

The respiratory system at rest, during exercise and during recovery

The mechanics of breathing

Table 6 shows the mechanics of breathing at rest and during exercise, as well as the muscles involved.

Table 6 The mechanics of breathing

Ventilation phase	Muscles used during breathing at rest	Muscles used during exercise
Inspiration	Diaphragm and external intercostals contract to increase the volume of the thoracic cavity and lower the air pressure	In addition to the diaphragm and external intercostals, extra muscles are used for inspiration (sternocleidomastoid and pectoralis minor) which increase the volume of the thoracic cavity even more, creating a greater pressure gradient, so that air enters the lungs more quickly
Expiration	In this passive process, the diaphragm and external intercostals just relax to reduce the volume of the thoracic cavity and increase air pressure	Internal intercostals and the abdominals are used for expiration, decreasing the volume of the thoracic cavity and increasing the pressure, so air is forced out of the lungs more quickly

Breathing rate, tidal volume and minute ventilation

Breathing rate, tidal volume and minute ventilation (Figure 5) are measures of the efficiency of the respiratory system. You need to know the measurements shown in Table 7 for your exam.

Table 7 Average breathing rate, tidal volume and minute ventilation for an untrained and trained performer at rest and maximal intensity

Lung volume or capacity	Definition	Resting value (untrained)	Maximal value (untrained)	Resting value (trained)	Maximal value (trained)
Breathing rate (f)	The number of times we breathe in or out per minute	12–15 breaths per minute	40–50 breaths per minute	11–12 breaths per minute	50–60 breaths per minute
Tidal volume (TV)	Volume of air breathed in or out per breath	500 ml per breath	2.5–3 l per breath	500 ml per breath	3–3.5 l per breath
Minute ventilation (VE)	Volume of air breathed in or out per minute	6–7.5 l per minute	100–150 l per minute	5.5–6 l per minute	150–160 l per minute

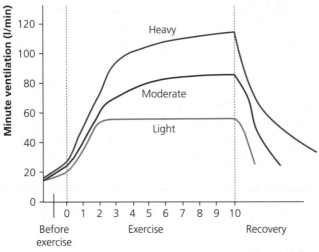

Figure 5 Minute ventilation (litres per minute) in response to exercise of light, moderate and heavy intensity

Gas transport

97% of the oxygen in the blood combines with haemoglobin to form oxyhaemoglobin and 3% dissolves in blood plasma. 70% of the carbon dioxide in blood dissolves in water and is transported as carbonic acid, 23% combines with haemoglobin and 7% dissolves in the blood plasma.

Gaseous exchange

External respiration

The structure of the alveoli is designed to help gaseous exchange:

- Thin walls result in a short **diffusion** pathway.
- An extensive capillary network surrounds the alveoli, providing an excellent blood supply.
- The huge surface area resulting from millions of alveoli in each lung allows for a greater uptake of oxygen.

Diffusion The movement of gas molecules from an area of high concentration or partial pressure to an area of low concentration or partial pressure.

The **partial pressure** of oxygen (pO_2) in the alveoli is higher than that in the capillary blood vessels. This is because oxygen has been removed by the working muscles, so its concentration in the blood is lower and therefore so is its partial pressure. The difference in partial pressure is referred to as the concentration/diffusion gradient and the bigger this gradient, the faster diffusion will be. Oxygen will diffuse from the alveoli into the blood until the pressure is equal in both. The movement of carbon dioxide occurs in the same way but in the reverse direction. This time the partial pressure of carbon dioxide (pCO_2) in the blood entering the alveolar capillaries is higher than in the alveoli, so carbon dioxide diffuses into the alveoli from the blood until the pressure is equal in both.

Internal respiration

In the capillary membranes surrounding the muscle the partial pressure of oxygen is higher than in the muscle, which allows oxygen to diffuse from the blood into the muscle until equilibrium is reached. Conversely, the partial pressure of carbon dioxide in the blood is lower than in the muscle, so again diffusion occurs and carbon dioxide moves into the blood to be transported to the lungs.

Oxyhaemoglobin dissociation curve

The oxyhaemoglobin dissociation curve represents the relationship between oxygen and haemoglobin (Figure 6). From this curve you can see that in the lungs there is almost full saturation (concentration) of oxyhaemoglobin, but at the tissues (muscles) the partial pressure of oxygen is lower because haemoglobin gives up some of its oxygen to the muscles and is therefore no longer fully saturated.

Partial pressure The pressure exerted by an individual gas when it exists within a mixture of gases.

Knowledge check 7

Explain how the gas exchange system operates at the muscles.

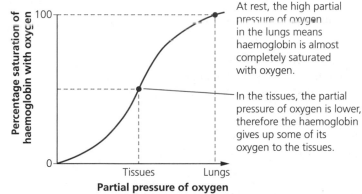

At rest, the high partial pressure of oxygen in the lungs means haemoglobin is almost completely saturated with oxygen.

In the tissues, the partial pressure of oxygen is lower, therefore the haemoglobin gives up some of its oxygen to the tissues.

Figure 6 The oxyhaemoglobin dissociation curve

During exercise this S-shaped curve shifts to the right, because when muscles require more oxygen the dissociation of oxygen from haemoglobin in the blood capillaries to the muscle tissue occurs more readily. This increases the volume of oxygen available for diffusion and therefore aerobic energy production for exercise.

This shift to the right is known as the **Bohr shift**. Three factors cause the Bohr shift:
- a decrease in blood pH (Figure 7)
- an increase in blood temperature
- an increase in blood carbon dioxide

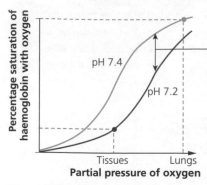

Figure 7 The effect of changing acidity on the oxyhaemoglobin dissociation curve

Neural and chemical regulation of breathing during physical activity and sport

The sympathetic nervous system increases breathing rate and the parasympathetic nervous system lowers breathing rate. The **respiratory control centre (RCC)** located in the medulla oblongata of the brain controls the rate and depth of breathing and uses both neural and chemical control. The RCC has two main areas: the inspiratory centre (IC) and the expiratory centre (EC). At rest the IC is responsible for the rhythmic cycle of breathing. Nerve impulses are generated via the intercostal nerve to the external intercostals and the phrenic nerve to the diaphragm in order for them to contract.

During exercise, blood acidity increases due to an increase in both the carbon dioxide concentration of plasma and lactic acid production. These changes are detected by chemoreceptors, which send impulses to the IC to increase breathing by recruiting additional inspiratory muscles (namely the sternocleidomastoid, scalenes and pectoralis minor) until blood acidity has returned to normal. As a result, the rate, depth and rhythm of breathing increases.

Stretch receptors are also activated during exercise, when breathing is deeper and the lungs are stretched further. Stretch receptors prevent over-inflation of the lungs by sending impulses to the EC, which then stimulates the expiratory muscles (rectus abdominus and internal intercostals) so that expiration occurs.

Other neural receptors include thermoreceptors which send impulses to the RCC about changes in blood temperature, and proprioceptors which send impulses to the RCC about motor activity in the muscles and joints.

Impact of physical activity on the respiratory system

Taking part in physical activity and sport, as part of a healthy lifestyle, can have a positive effect on the respiratory system:

- It improves the efficiency of the respiratory system, so the body can supply muscles with more oxygen due to an increase in the surface area and capillary density of the alveoli.
- Respiratory muscles are strengthened, resulting in deeper breathing.
- Increased gaseous exchange occurs, so more oxygen diffuses into the blood and more carbon dioxide diffuses from the blood.
- Tidal volume and minute ventilation increase, allowing more oxygen to diffuse into the muscles and carbon dioxide to diffuse out.

Respiratory control centre (RCC) Located in the medulla oblongata of the brain, it controls the rate of ventilation.

Summary

After studying this topic you should be able to:
- understand the key roles of the cardiovascular and respiratory systems at rest, during exercise and during recovery
- interpret relevant data and graphs and show a knowledge of heart rate, stroke volume and cardiac output
- explain the cardiac cycle (diastole and systole) and conduction system
- describe neural, hormonal and intrinsic control of heart rate
- explain the vascular shunt mechanism and give the role of the vasomotor control centre, arterioles and pre-capillary sphincters
- describe the mechanisms of venous return
- understand the mechanics of breathing
- explain neural and chemical control of breathing
- explain gaseous exchange at the alveoli and muscles, using diffusion and pressure gradients
- define and apply breathing frequency, tidal volume and minute ventilation
- explain the dissociation of oxyhaemoglobin

Energy for exercise

Adenosine triphosphate and energy transfer

Adenosine triphosphate (ATP) is the 'energy currency' found in our body cells, and is the source of energy we use for muscle contractions. When broken down it releases its stored energy. ATP in the muscle cell is quickly exhausted (as ATP cannot be stored) so we have to constantly rebuild ATP by converting ADP (adenosine diphosphate) and P (phosphate) back into ATP using phosphocreatine, carbohydrates, fats and protein in one of three energy systems (see below). The breakdown and resynthesis of ATP is a **coupled reaction**:

$$ATP \rightarrow ADP + P + energy$$

$$ADP + P + energy \rightarrow ATP$$

Energy is released from ATP when the bonds that hold this compound together are broken down by the enzyme ATPase, in an **exothermic reaction**:

$$ATP \xrightarrow{ATPase} ADP + P + energy$$

Rebuilding or resynthesising ATP from ADP and P is an **endothermic reaction**.

Energy systems and ATP resynthesis

There are three energy systems that break down chemical/food fuels to provide the energy for ATP resynthesis. Table 8 outlines the knowledge you need in your exam for each system.

Coupled reaction A reaction in which energy is transferred from one side to the other.

Exothermic reaction A reaction in which energy is released.

Endothermic reaction A reaction that needs energy to work.

Table 8 The key descriptors, strengths and weaknesses of the ATP-PC, glycolytic and aerobic systems

Knowledge for your exam	ATP-PC system	Glycolytic system	Aerobic system
Type of reaction	Anaerobic	Anaerobic	Aerobic
Chemical or food fuel used	Phosphocreatine (PC)	Glycogen/glucose	Glycogen/glucose/free fatty acids
Specific site of the reaction	Sarcoplasm	Sarcoplasm	Stage 1: anaerobic glycolysis — sarcoplasm Stage 2: Krebs cycle — matrix of the mitochondria Stage 3: electron transport chain — cristae of the mitochondria
Controlling enzyme	Creatine kinase	Glycogen phosphorylase, phosphofructokinase (PFK), lactate dehydrogenase	Glycogen phosphorylase, phosphofructokinase (PFK), coenzyme A and lipase
ATP yield	1 mole of PC yields 1 mole of ATP	1 mole of glycogen yields 2 moles of ATP	1 mole of glycogen yields up to 38 moles of ATP
Specific stages within the system	PC $\rightarrow$ P + C + energy (exothermic) energy + P + ADP $\rightarrow$ ATP (endothermic)	Anaerobic glycolysis: glycogen/glucose $\rightarrow$ pyruvic acid + energy Lactate pathway: pyruvic acid $\rightarrow$ lactic acid energy + 2P + 2ADP $\rightarrow$ 2ATP (endothermic)	Aerobic glycolysis, Kreb's cycle and electron transport chain (ETC): glucose + $6O_2 \rightarrow 6CO_2 + 6H_2O$ + energy (exothermic) energy + 38P + 38ADP $\rightarrow$ 38ATP (endothermic)
By-products	None	Lactic acid	H_2O and CO_2
Strengths	ATP can be resynthesised rapidly using the ATP-PC system There are no fatiguing by-products It is possible to extend the time for the ATP-PC system through use of creatine supplementation	ATP can be resynthesised quite quickly due to very few chemical reactions In the presence of oxygen, lactic acid can be converted back into liver glycogen or used as a fuel through oxidation into carbon dioxide and water Provides energy for high-intensity activity for longer than the ATP-PC system — up to 3 minutes	More ATP can be produced (38 ATP) There are no fatiguing by-products (carbon dioxide and water) Lots of glycogen and triglyceride stores, so exercise can last for a long time
Weaknesses	There is only a limited supply of PC in each muscle cell — it can only last for 8–10 seconds Only 1 mole of ATP can be resynthesised through one mole of PC PC resynthesis can only take place in the presence of oxygen (i.e. when the intensity of the exercise is reduced)	Lactic acid is the by-product The accumulation of acid in the body denatures enzymes and prevents them increasing the rate at which chemical reactions take place	This is a complicated system, so cannot be used straightaway It takes a while for enough oxygen to become available to meet the demands of the activity and to ensure that glycogen and fatty acids are completely broken down Fatty acid transportation to muscles is low and also requires 15% more oxygen to be broken down than glycogen

Energy continuum of physical activity

Energy continuum is a term that describes the type of respiration used by physical activities. Whether it is aerobic or anaerobic respiration depends on the intensity and duration of the exercise (see Figure 8 and Table 9).

The **energy continuum** explains the contribution of each energy system to overall energy production, depending on the intensity and duration of the activity.

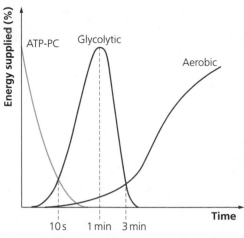

Figure 8 The energy continuum related to exercise duration

Table 9 Energy system used according to intensity and duration of exercise

Duration of performance	Intensity	Energy supplied by
Less than 10 seconds	Very high	ATP-PC
8–90 seconds	High to very high	ATP-PC and anaerobic glycolytic
90 seconds to 3 minutes	High	Anaerobic glycolytic and aerobic
3+ minutes	Low to medium	Aerobic

Intermittent exercise

Intermittent exercise is where there are both work and relief periods, for example in interval training or in a game where there are different intensities of exercise — from walking to jogging to sprinting. In a game of football, for instance, a player may sprint onto a ball, jog to keep up with play, jump to head a ball, tackle and walk during the setting up of a free kick. This means that there are various physiological demands placed on the player throughout a match, and as a result they will use different energy systems accordingly. The threshold of an energy system occurs when the system can no longer provide energy, so there is a switch to another system. Thresholds for each energy system are shown in Figure 9.

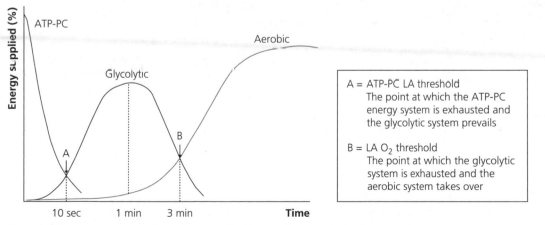

A = ATP-PC LA threshold
The point at which the ATP-PC energy system is exhausted and the glycolytic system prevails

B = LA O_2 threshold
The point at which the glycolytic system is exhausted and the aerobic system takes over

Figure 9 The percentage of energy supplied by each energy system over time

Recovery periods

Some team games, such as basketball, are predominantly anaerobic and rely heavily on the ATP-PC and the glycolytic systems. It is important for these players to try to replenish PC stores in any recovery period they have, such as a timeout, because they can be replenished quickly: 50% in 30 seconds and 100% in 3 minutes. Similarly, oxygen stored in myoglobin only takes up to 3 minutes to be fully replenished.

If demands are too high for the glycolytic system to produce energy, then blood lactate levels will rise dramatically. It is possible to break down and remove any lactic acid with the correct work–relief ratio when oxygen levels are high. In addition, quarter- and half-time breaks provide an opportunity for rehydration and glycogen replenishment.

Fitness level

When blood lactate values go above 4 mmol of lactic acid per litre of blood, onset of blood lactate accumulation (OBLA) has been reached. The fitter the performer, the more OBLA can be delayed because they can work at a higher percentage of their VO_2 max (see p. 32) and also tolerate higher levels of lactic acid more effectively. This is called **buffering**.

Buffering A process that aids the removal of lactate and maintains acidity levels in the blood and muscle.

Knowledge check 8

For each of the following examples in a game of football, which energy system would be the predominant energy provider?

(a) A short, 10 m sprint into space to receive the ball.

(b) Making a quick break in attack over the length of the pitch.

(c) Jogging to keep in position.

The recovery process

The recovery process is how the body returns to its pre-exercise state. At the end of exercise, a performer breathes heavily, and this breathlessness is a result of **EPOC**, whereby extra oxygen is taken in and used to restore normal conditions.

EPOC The amount of O_2 consumed during recovery above that which is normally consumed at rest.

Conditions which can be restored to normal quickly form the fast replenishment stage (alactacid component). This involves the restoration of ATP and PC together with the resaturation of myoglobin with oxygen. Restoration of PC takes up to three minutes for 100% or 30 seconds for 50% and uses 2–3 litres of oxygen. Myoglobin replenishment takes up to 2 minutes and uses 0.5 litres of oxygen.

The slow replenishment stage (lactacid component) concerns the removal of lactic acid. This can take an hour or more and is achieved by oxidising lactic acid into carbon dioxide and water, so the lactic acid is used as an energy source. It can also be converted into glycogen, glucose and protein and removed through sweat and urine. Within this stage, heart rate, respiratory rate and body temperature all remain elevated.

Knowledge check 9

What are the functions of the alactacid component?

The effect of exercise intensity on EPOC and implications of the recovery process on training

The higher the intensity of exercise, the larger the **oxygen deficit**, resulting in faster lactate accumulation. This results in a greater EPOC and the performer being more out of breath.

Oxygen deficit When there is not enough oxygen available at the start of exercise to provide all the energy aerobically.

When training it is important to perform an active cool-down, which maintains respiratory and heart rates and flushes the muscle and capillary beds with oxygenated blood. This speeds up the removal of lactic acid and reduces the length of the slow lactacid component of EPOC.

Cooling aids can be used during recovery to also speed up lactic acid removal and reduce muscle soreness and DOMS, allowing the performer to be ready for the next training session. Anaerobic training will also boost the efficiency of the fast component as ATP and PC stores have to be continually replenished.

Summary

After studying this topic you should be able to:
- demonstrate knowledge and understanding of the role of adenosine triphosphate (ATP) as an energy currency and its resynthesis during exercise
- demonstrate knowledge of the type of reaction chemical or food fuel used, specific site of the reaction, controlling enzyme, ATP yield, specific stages and by-products for each of the three energy systems — ATP-PC, glycolytic and aerobic
- understand when each of the energy systems is used according to the intensity and duration of exercise (energy continuum)
- understand the recovery process and the implications of this for training

Environmental effects on body systems

Environmental conditions can affect the efficiency of the cardiovascular and respiratory systems and therefore impact on performance.

Exercise at altitude

At high **altitude** the partial pressure of oxygen is lower even though the air still contains approximately 21% oxygen. This results in haemoglobin not being fully saturated, which lowers the oxygen carrying capacity of the blood.

Altitude The height of an area of land above sea level, with 'high altitude' usually considered to be over 2500 m above sea level.

Effect of altitude on the cardiovascular and respiratory systems

The effects of high altitude on the cardiovascular and respiratory systems combine to reduce aerobic capacity and VO_2 max, impacting on the intensity and duration of an athlete's performance:
- Ventilation increases both at rest and during exercise to maintain oxygen consumption.
- The oxygen diffusion gradient is reduced.
- Blood volume decreases because plasma volume decreases by 25% to accommodate an increase in red blood cell density.
- Stroke volume decreases, which increases heart rate.

> **Exam tip**
>
> High altitude has most impact on endurance performers. Anaerobic performers, such as 100 m sprinters, are mostly unaffected.

Acclimatisation

Acclimatisation is essential prior to a competition at high altitude in order to minimise the impact of the decreased partial pressure of oxygen. Acclimatisation starts immediately on arrival at altitude, but at first there is a negative impact on performance as the athlete struggles to cope with the lower partial pressure of oxygen. However, after 1–2 weeks at an altitude above 2400 m the athlete will start to see benefits for the cardiovascular and respiratory systems, including:

- an increase in red blood cells due to an increase in the secretion of the hormone **EPO**
- an increased concentration of haemoglobin
- increased blood viscosity and capillarisation
- enhanced oxygen transport and increased lactate tolerance

However, it is also important to weigh up the disadvantages associated with high altitude and to prepare for them accordingly. The performer could suffer from altitude sickness, poor sleep and headaches, but with acclimatisation this should improve. Detraining will occur because training intensity has to be reduced when the performer first arrives at altitude due to the decreased availability of oxygen. Therefore, correct timing of arrival before an important competition is crucial.

EPO (erythropoietin) A hormone that controls red blood cell production.

Knowledge check 10

Why is it important for an endurance athlete to acclimatise for a competition at high altitude?

Exercise in the heat

Temperature regulation

Thermoreceptors detect increases in temperature in hot conditions and send impulses to the thermoregulatory centre located in the medulla oblongata in the brain. This causes the blood vessels near the surface of the skin to vasodilate and heat evaporates through sweating. Heat is also lost by radiation, convection and conduction. Failure to regulate body temperature in hot conditions can have a negative impact on performance.

Under exercise conditions, with muscle contractions producing further heat, core body temperature increases further. A performer who fails to regulate heat can enter **hyperthermia**. When a performer overheats, blood volume decreases, leading to a decrease in venous return, stroke volume, cardiac output and blood pressure. This affects blood flow and the amount of oxygen muscles receive. In addition, sweating becomes less efficient and **dehydration** occurs. Effects on the respiratory system include drying of the airways, which makes breathing more difficult and decreases gaseous exchange. Breathing frequency therefore increases in an attempt to meet oxygen demand.

Hyperthermia When body temperature rises significantly.

Dehydration The loss of water from body tissues.

Cardiovascular drift

Cardiovascular drift occurs where there is an increase in heart rate and a decrease in stroke volume (Figure 10). It occurs after 10 minutes in warm conditions and is caused by a reduction of fluid in the blood plasma due to an increase in sweating. The blood becomes more viscous and consequently venous return decreases, so heart rate increases to maintain cardiac output.

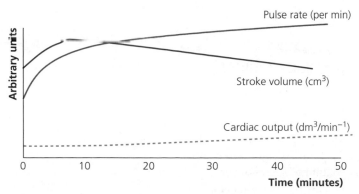

Figure 10 Graph of cardiovascular drift

To maximise performance in heat and humidity it is important to acclimatise the body for 7–14 days to increase tolerance to heat. Cooling aids such as ice vests reduce core body temperature and delay the effects of dehydration. During and after competition, performers should rehydrate with a hypotonic or isotonic drink to replace lost fluids, glucose and electrolytes.

Exam tip

Endurance-based physical activities are affected more by heat than explosive and maximal events, which are relatively unaffected.

Summary

After studying this topic you should be able to:
- explain the effect of altitude on the cardiovascular and respiratory systems
- understand the importance of acclimatisation and the timing of arrival at altitude
- explain the effect of heat on the cardiovascular and respiratory systems, including temperature regulation and cardiovascular drift

■ Exercise physiology

Diet and nutrition and their effect on physical activity and sport

Diet and nutrition

A healthy, balanced diet is important to support a training programme. For 19–50 year olds, the government recommends 2500 calories per day for men and 2000 calories per day for women. Typically, a balanced diet should contain 55% carbohydrate, 15% protein and no more than 30% fats. In addition, at least five portions of fruit and vegetables should be consumed per day.

Carbohydrates

Carbohydrates are the principal source of energy used by the body. Glycogen and glucose provide the fuel for both aerobic and anaerobic energy production. Glucose is stored in the muscles and liver as glycogen, but these stores are limited, so regular refuelling is necessary. Surplus glucose, for example from a high-sugar diet, will be converted into triglycerides (the main constituents of body fat in humans) and stored in the body as fat.

Proteins

Proteins are found in large quantities in meat, eggs, milk and soya. Amino acids from proteins are important for muscle growth and repair and are used to make enzymes, hormones and haemoglobin. Proteins are a minor source of energy and tend to be used more by power athletes, who have a greater need to repair and develop muscle tissue. They can also be used as a fuel (when carbohydrates and fats are depleted).

Fats

Fats can only be broken down for aerobic energy production but have twice the energy yield of carbohydrates. They also insulate nerves, form cell membranes and cushion organs. They provide essential fatty acids and allow absorption of the fat-soluble vitamins A, D, E and K.

Too many saturated fatty acids, for example in butter and bacon, lead to weight gain, which can affect stamina, limit flexibility and lead to health problems, such as coronary heart disease, diabetes and high blood pressure. Unsaturated fatty acids, for example as found in avocados, are important for boosting oxygen delivery and reducing inflammation and joint stiffness.

Minerals

Minerals are essential inorganic nutrients that are required in small quantities to maintain healthy body functions. They are found in meat, cereals, fish, dairy foods, vegetables, fruit and nuts. Examples are given in Table 10.

Exam tip

Make sure you are able to link carbohydrates, fats and proteins with performance in different activities and sports, as well as with the relevant energy systems.

Carbohydrates A food group that includes sugars, such as those in fruit, and starches, for example in potatoes. They circulate in the bloodstream as glucose, or are stored as glycogen in the muscles and liver.

Proteins Provide amino acids that are essential for the growth and repair of cells and tissues.

Fats Triglycerides, which provide the body with fatty acids for energy production.

Minerals Inorganic nutrients that we get from foods and which are essential for healthy body functions.

Table 10 How minerals help performance in physical activity and sport

Mineral	Exercise-related function
Calcium	For strong bones and teeth and for efficient nerve and muscle function
Sodium	Regulates fluid levels in the body; too much can lead to an increase in blood pressure, which increases risk of a stroke/heart attack
Iron	Used to form haemoglobin in red blood cells, which transports oxygen; lack of iron leads to anaemia
Phosphorus	Important for bone health and energy production

Vitamins

Vitamins are essential to maintain healthy body functions. They can be consumed in adequate quantities through a balanced diet. Table 11 summarises some different vitamins and their uses in the body.

Table 11 Different vitamins and their uses in the body

Vitamin	Essential for …
A	Antioxidant properties; eye health, cell and bone growth
D	Bone health; protection against cancer and heart disease
E	Antioxidant properties; skin, eye and immune system health
K	Blood clotting and bone health
C	Skin, blood vessel, soft tissue and bone health
B	Breakdown of food, haemoglobin formation, and skin, eye and nervous system health

Water

Water transports nutrients, hormones and waste products around the body and regulates body temperature. Blood plasma is 90% water and carries glucose to the respiring muscles. During exercise water is lost in the cooling down process. A lack of water pre, during or post exercise can cause dehydration, and this can result in decreased plasma volume and stroke volume and increased temperature and heart rate. As a result, performance will deteriorate.

Fibre

Fibre is found in cereals, bread, beans, lentils, fruit and vegetables, and is important during exercise because it can slow down the time it takes the body to break down food, which results in a slower, more sustained release of energy. Dietary fibre creates bulk in the small intestine, helping to prevent constipation and aiding digestion.

Energy intake, expenditure and balance in physical activity and performance

The nutritional needs of an elite performer will vary according to the demands of the activity performed. It is crucial that sports performers meet their **energy** needs during periods of training to improve performance while maintaining health. Failure to consume sufficient calories can result in muscle loss (atrophy), decreased intensity and duration of performance, slower recovery rates and increased risk of fatigue, injury and illness.

Energy intake

Energy intake is the total amount of energy from food and drinks consumed, measured in joules or calories. An athlete's diet may differ significantly depending on the intensity and duration of their activity.

Vitamins Organic compounds that the body needs in small amounts for a range of essential processes.

Knowledge check 11

How might the diet of a sedentary individual differ from that of an endurance athlete and a power athlete?

Energy The ability to perform work. It is measured in joules or calories, where 1 calorie equates to 4.18 joules.

Energy expenditure

Energy expenditure is the sum of **basal metabolic rate (BMR)**, the **thermic effect of food (TEF)** and the energy expended in physical activity.

Physical activity energy expenditure is the total number of calories required to perform daily tasks. One method of recording the additional energy expenditure of physical activity is the **metabolic equivalent task (MET)**. This monitors oxygen consumption during exercise and this value is then compared with resting oxygen uptake. 1 MET (1 kcal/kg/h) is energy expenditure at rest. Activities with a MET score of 3.0–5.9 are classed as moderate exercise and 6.0 METS and above as high-intensity activity.

Energy balance

Energy balance is the relationship between energy intake and energy expenditure:

- energy in > energy expenditure = weight gain
- energy in < energy expenditure = weight loss
- energy in = energy expenditure = weight stays the same

Ergogenic aids

Ergogenic aids are used to improve performance in sport.

Pharmacological aids

Pharmacological aids are drugs that are taken to improve performance. They can be either legal or illegal. For your exam you need to know the benefits and risks of the illegal pharmacological aids shown in Table 12.

Table 12 The potential benefits and risks of pharmacological aids

Pharmacological aid	Potential benefits	Potential risks
Anabolic steroids — synthetic hormones that resemble the male hormone testosterone and are taken illegally by some power athletes	Increased muscle mass and strength Increased speed of recovery Increased intensity and duration of training	Irritability, aggression and mood swings Liver damage and potential heart failure Acne and hormonal disturbances
Erythropoietin (EPO) — a natural hormone in the body that produces red blood cells; RhEPO can be taken artificially to boost oxygen levels, and is used illegally by some endurance performers	Increased red blood cell and haemoglobin count Increased oxygen transport and aerobic capacity Increased intensity and duration of performance before fatigue	Increased blood viscosity Decreased cardiac output Increased risk of blood clots and heart failure Decreased natural production of EPO
Human growth hormone (HGH) — a synthetic product that mimics the naturally produced growth hormone, which is used illegally by some power athletes	Increased muscle mass and strength Increased fat metabolism and decreased fat mass Increased blood glucose levels Increased speed of recovery Increased intensity and duration of training	Abnormal bone and muscle development Enlargement of the vital organs, potentially leading to multi-organ failure Increased risk of certain cancers and diabetes

Basal metabolic rate (BMR) The amount of energy your body burns at rest.

Thermic effect of food (TEF) The amount of energy required to digest and process the food we eat.

Physical activity energy expenditure The total number of calories required to perform daily tasks.

Metabolic equivalent task (MET) The ratio of a performer's working metabolic rate to their resting metabolic rate.

Knowledge check 12

How would an athlete calculate their overall energy expenditure?

Knowledge check 13

Evaluate the use of anabolic steroids to improve a sprinter's performance in the 100m.

Physiological aids

For your exam you need to know the benefits and risks of the physiological aids shown in Table 13.

Table 13 The potential benefits and risks of physiological aids

Physiological aid	Potential benefits	Potential risks
Blood doping is illegal and is used by some endurance athletes. It involves increasing the red blood cell volume. Blood is removed 4–6 weeks before competition and frozen. The body then compensates, replenishing lost RBCs, and a few hours before the event the blood is infused back into the body.	Increase in RBCs and therefore more haemoglobin for transportation of O_2 Increased O_2 transport and aerobic capacity Increased intensity and duration of performance	Increased blood viscosity Decreased cardiac output Increased risk of blood clots and heart disease Risk of transfusion infections, such as hepatitis and HIV
Intermittent hypoxic training (IHT). Similar to altitude training, but an athlete lives at sea level and trains wearing a mask supplying low ppO$_2$. This would benefit endurance performers.	Allows acclimatisation for events at altitude Increase in RBCs and therefore more haemoglobin for transportation of O_2 Increased intensity and duration before fatigue Increase in mitochondria and buffering capacity, and therefore a delay in OBLA	Any benefit is quickly lost when IHT stops May lose motivation and disrupt training patterns Hard to reach normal work rates Decreased immune function and increased risk of infection Dehydration
Cooling aids: Pre-event — ice vests, cold towel wraps, used 10–00 minutes before to reduce core body temperature Injury — ice packs, sprays, PRICE (protect, rest, ice, compression, elevate) Post-event — ice baths to speed up recovery	Reduced core body temperature decreases sweating and dehydration and delays fatigue Decreased injury pain and swelling Increased speed of recovery and repair Decreased DOMS	Difficult to perceive exercise intensity due to ice burns and pain May mask or worsen injuries Chest pain and decreased efficiency in the elderly Dangerous for those with heart and blood pressure problems

Knowledge check 14

What would a performer need to consider when blood doping?

Nutritional aids

Food

The amount of food an athlete eats is important in order to meet the energy balance required to maintain health, training and performance quality. Recommendations for an athlete training intensely for more than 4 hours a day are a carbohydrate intake of 10–12 g per kg per day. The content and timing of pre- and post-event high-carbohydrate meals are also important. A pre-event meal should take place 3 hours before an event and consist of slow-digesting carbohydrates, such as porridge oats or beans, to maximise glycogen stores and prevent glycogen depletion. 1–2 hours before the event a smaller, fast-digesting meal should be consumed to maintain glucose levels. It is also important to avoid eating carbohydrates immediately before an event as the body may try to counteract the raised glucose levels and become dizzy or fatigued. A post-event meal should be consumed within 2 hours but ideally within 30 minutes of finishing. Fast-digesting carbohydrates, such as a chocolate milkshake, are easy to consume so soon after exercise and will result in faster recovery.

Hydration

An athlete should keep hydrated prior to performance and replace all lost fluids after the event. Electrolytes lost through sweat must also be replaced. A lack of water pre, during or post exercise can cause dehydration, and this can result in decreased plasma volume and stroke volume, increased temperature and heart rate, and a decrease in performance. Sports drinks (isotonic and hypotonic) contain glucose and electrolytes, and these can be used to rehydrate and supply glucose for energy production. Hypertonic drinks have a higher glucose concentration and can be used during recovery.

Glycogen/carbo-loading

Glycogen/carbo-loading is a form of dietary manipulation to increase glycogen stores over and above that which can normally be stored (**supercompensation**).

Method one: 6 days before competition the performer eats a diet high in protein for 3 days and exercises at relatively high intensity to burn off any existing carbohydrate stores. This is followed by 3 days of a diet high in carbohydrates and some light training. The theory is that by totally depleting glycogen stores they can then be increased by up to two times the original amount (supercompensation) and can prevent a performer from 'hitting the wall'.

Method two: 1 day before competition, 3 minutes of high-intensity exercise opens a 'carbo window'. Replenishing glycogen stores during the first 20 minutes of this window after exercise can enhance performance the next day. In the 20 minutes immediately after exercise the body is most able to restore lost glycogen. The 'carbo window' closes after 2 hours.

Method three: a non-depletion protocol, where training intensity is reduced the week before competition. Then 3 days before competition a high-carbohydrate diet is followed with light-intensity exercise.

Disadvantages during the carbo-loading phase are that performers may experience water retention, bloating, heavy legs and weight increase, and during the depletion phase irritability and a lack of energy.

Creatine

Creatine is a supplement used to increase the amount of phosphocreatine stored in the muscles. Phosphocreatine is used to fuel the ATP-PC system, which provides energy. Increasing the amount of creatine in the muscles will allow this energy system to last longer. It can also help improve muscle mass and recovery times. Creatine is most suitable for athletes in explosive events such as sprinting. Negative side effects are bloating, muscle cramps, diarrhoea, water retention and vomiting. There is also mixed evidence for its benefits.

Caffeine

Caffeine is a naturally occurring stimulant, which can increase mental alertness and reduce fatigue. It is also thought to improve the mobilisation of fatty acids in the body, thereby sparing muscle glycogen stores. It is used by endurance performers who predominantly rely on the aerobic system, since fats are the preferred fuel for low-intensity, long-endurance exercise. However, caffeine can lead to a loss of fine control, dehydration, insomnia, muscle cramps, vomiting and diarrhoea.

Sodium bicarbonate

Sodium bicarbonate is an antacid. It can increase the buffering capacity of the blood, so it can neutralise the negative effects of lactic acid and hydrogen ions that are produced in the muscles during high-intensity activity, thus delaying fatigue. Negative side effects include vomiting, pain, cramping, diarrhoea and feeling bloated.

Nitrate

Nitrates are inorganic compounds that can dilate blood vessels, reduce blood pressure, increase blood flow to the tissues, reduce the oxygen 'cost' of exercise and aid recovery. Risks include headaches, dizziness or light-headedness. The long-term effects on health are unclear, and there is a possible carcinogenic risk.

Summary

After studying this topic you should be able to:
- identify the components of a healthy, balanced diet, namely carbohydrates, proteins, fats, minerals, vitamins, fibre and water, and explain their functions
- explain energy intake and expenditure and energy balance in physical activity and performance
- outline the benefits and risks of anabolic steroids, erythropoietin (EPO) and human growth hormone (HGH)
- explain the benefits and risks of blood doping, intermittent hypoxic training (IHT) and cooling aids
- identify the amount and composition of food that a sports performer should eat, as well as the timing of meals and hydration
- outline the use of nutritional supplements such as glycogen/carbo-loading, creatine, caffeine, sodium bicarbonate and nitrate, and explain how they help improve performance

Preparation and training methods

Developing personal health and fitness programmes

When developing health and fitness programmes for aerobic strength and flexibility training it is important to first select an appropriate fitness test in order to chart improvement and make sure that each session includes a warm-up and a cool-down. It is also important to consider the principles of training so that progression is made. There are several versions of the principles of training. This guide uses SPORR and FITT.

SPORR principles

Specificity — choosing the relevant training (same energy system, muscle fibre type, skills and movements).

Progressive overload — gradually training harder throughout a training programme as fitness improves (heavier weights, longer training sessions, greater distances).

Reversibility — often referred to as detraining; stop and the level of fitness deteriorates.

Recovery — rest days are needed to allow the body to recover from training.

FITT principles

Frequency — to improve you need to train more often.

Intensity — you must train harder.

Time spent training — this needs to gradually increase.

Type of exercise — using different forms of exercise maintains motivation but the type chosen needs to be relevant to your chosen activity.

Periodisation of training

Periodisation involves dividing the training year into blocks or sections in which specific training occurs. There are three main cycles:

- A **macrocycle** is a long-term performance goal, which can be divided into:
  - the preparation period — similar to pre-season training, where fitness is developed
  - the competition period — the performance period, where skills and techniques are refined
  - the transition period — the end of the season, where rest and recovery take place
- A **mesocycle** is usually a 4–12 week period of training with a particular focus, such as power. A 100 m sprinter, for example, will focus on power, reaction time and speed.
- A **microcycle** is a plan for 1 week or a few days of training that is repeated throughout the length of the mesocycle.

Tapering involves reducing the volume and/or intensity of training prior to competition. Planning and organising training in this way prepares the athlete both physically and mentally for a major competition, and allows peaking to occur.

Aerobic training

Aerobic capacity and maximal oxygen uptake (VO₂ max)

Aerobic capacity is a key fitness component that is dependent on the efficiency of the cardiovascular, respiratory and muscular systems. It is important for success in any endurance-based performance.

A key component of aerobic capacity is **VO₂ max**, which is measured in millilitres per kilogram per minute (ml/kg/min). An untrained individual will have an average VO_2 max of around 40–50 ml/kg/min, with a highly trained athlete at around 90 ml/kg/min. A good VO_2 max allows a performer to work at a higher intensity for longer because they can utilise oxygen more effectively.

Factors affecting VO₂ max

The following structural/physiological characteristics will enable a performer to have a higher VO_2 max:

- increased maximum cardiac output
- increased stroke volume/ejection fraction/cardiac hypertrophy
- greater heart rate range
- increased levels of haemoglobin and red blood cell count

Knowledge check 16

How can frequency be applied to a training programme?

Knowledge check 17

What are the three cycles used in periodisation?

Aerobic capacity
The ability of the body to inspire, transport and utilise oxygen to perform sustained periods of aerobic activity.

VO₂ max The maximum volume of oxygen that can be taken up and used by the muscles per minute.

- increased stores of glycogen and triglycerides
- increased myoglobin content
- increased capillarisation around the muscles
- increased number and size of mitochondria
- increased surface area of alveoli
- increased lactate tolerance
- reduced body fat
- slow-twitch hypertrophy

Other general factors can affect VO_2 max:

- Lifestyle — smoking, sedentary lifestyle, poor diet and low fitness can all reduce VO_2 max.
- Training — VO_2 max can be improved by up to 10–20% following a period of aerobic training.
- Genetics — VO_2 max is largely genetically determined, which limits the impact of training.
- Gender — men generally have a VO_2 max that is approximately 20% higher than that of women.
- Age — as we get older VO_2 max declines as our body systems become less efficient.
- Body composition — a higher percentage of body fat decreases VO_2 max.

Methods of evaluating aerobic capacity

For your exam you need knowledge of the following tests.

Direct gas analysis

Direct gas analysis is an accurate and reliable method because it is carried out in laboratory conditions, and can be used for different types of exercise, for example running or cycling. However, it does require specialist equipment and is a maximal test to exhaustion, so not suitable for those with health problems.

NCF multi-stage fitness test

This is a 20 m progressive shuttle run producing results that can be compared with standardised tables. It is a simple, cheap test for large groups but only gives a prediction of VO_2 max. It is not sport specific because it only involves running, and as a maximal test there could be problems with motivation, and it may not suitable for everyone on health grounds.

Queen's college step test

This involves stepping on and off a box for 3 minutes at a height of 41.3 cm, with heart rate recovery used to predict results. It is a submaximal test for large groups, with published tables of normative data, that is simple and cheap to administer. However, it is only a predictor of VO_2 max, not sport specific and shorter subjects might be at a disadvantage.

Cooper 12-minute run

This involves covering as much distance as possible in 12 minutes and has the same advantages and disadvantages as the NCF multi-stage fitness test.

Exam tip

Make sure you can explain how these factors have an impact on VO_2 max.

Direct gas analysis measures the concentration of oxygen that is inspired and the concentration of carbon dioxide that is expired.

Intensity and duration of training to develop aerobic capacity

Continuous training

This training method is used by endurance performers and involves non-stop activity, such as jogging or cycling, for a duration of 20–80 minutes and at low to medium intensity (60–80% of max HR).

High-intensity interval training (HIIT)

This involves short intervals of anaerobic, maximum-intensity exercise (80–95% of maximum HR) followed by a recovery interval of aerobic exercise. It develops aerobic capacity but in a shorter time period than continuous training. It can be adapted according to fitness level, but care needs to be taken for those with health conditions.

The use of target heart rates as an intensity guide

It is important to train at the correct intensity to gain aerobic adaptations, and the use of target heart rates facilitates this (Figure 11).

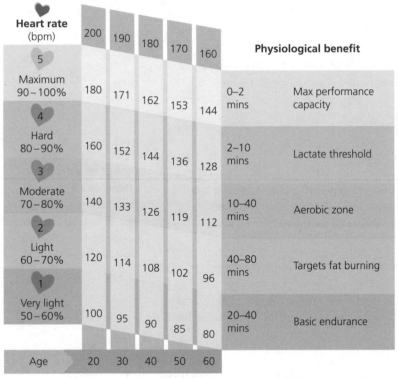

Figure 11 Heart rate training zones

Another method is Karvonen's Principle, which is more accurate because it takes into account a performer's age and resting HR, and uses the following formula:

training HR = resting HR + (% max HR × (max HR − resting HR))

For example, for an 18 year old with a resting HR of 66, training at 75%:

training HR = 66 + (0.75 × (202 − 66))

= 66 + 102

= 168 bpm

> **Exam tip**
>
> Fartlek training is another type of continuous training, which is interspersed with varied higher-intensity exercise, for example short sprints during a continuous run.

> **Knowledge check 18**
>
> Why is fartlek training a relevant method of training for a games player?

Physiological adaptations from aerobic training

Regular aerobic training over a period of at least 12 weeks will result in **physiological adaptations** to the cardiovascular, respiratory, musculoskeletal and metabolic systems.

Adaptations to the cardiovascular and respiratory systems will mean that the muscles will receive more oxygen. This will mean that a performer can work harder aerobically for longer, reducing the onset of fatigue and delaying OBLA. Table 14 identifies the cardiovascular and respiratory adaptations that occur as a result of aerobic training, and how they help improve aerobic capacity.

Physiological adaptations Changes the body makes as a result of exercise.

Table 14 The adaptations of the cardiovascular and respiratory systems after a period of aerobic training

Cardiovascular adaptations	How they help improve aerobic capacity
Cardiac hypertrophy	Increased stroke volume, which increases the oxygen carrying capacity of the blood Bradycardia
Increased elasticity of arterial walls	Increases the efficiency of the vascular shunt mechanism
Increased blood/plasma volume	Lower blood viscosity, which aids blood flow
Increase in the number of red blood cells and haemoglobin content	Increased oxygen carrying capacity of the blood and increased gaseous exchange
Capillarisation at the alveoli/muscles	Increased gaseous exchange
Respiratory adaptations	How they help improve aerobic capacity
Strengthened respiratory muscles	Increased efficiency of gaseous exchange Increased tidal volume and minute ventilation
Increase in the surface area of alveoli	Increased gaseous exchange

Knowledge check 19

How does a period of continuous training affect stroke volume and heart rate?

Musculoskeletal adaptations lead to an increase in aerobic respiration and in joint stability. Table 15 identifies the musculoskeletal adaptations that occur as a result of aerobic training, and how they help improve aerobic capacity.

Table 15 The adaptations of the musculoskeletal system after a period of aerobic training

Musculoskeletal adaptations	How they help improve aerobic capacity
Slow oxidative muscle fibre hypertrophy	Increases aerobic energy production and delays fatigue
Increased size and density of mitochondria	More aerobic respiration can take place
Increased levels of myoglobin	More oxygen can be stored in the muscles
Increased stores of glycogen and triglycerides	Increases duration of aerobic energy production
Increased strength of connective tissue (ligaments/tendons)	Increases joint stability/reduces injury
Increased thickness of articular cartilage	Increases joint lubrication through increased synovial production
Increased bone mineral density	Increases calcium absorption, leading to increased bone strength

Metabolic adaptations include an increase in the activity of aerobic enzymes, which increases glycogen and triglyceride metabolism, resulting in more fuel for the aerobic system. This therefore reduces the onset of fatigue. There is also a decrease in fat mass, which increases metabolic rate, and decreased insulin resistance, which improves glucose tolerance.

Strength training

Types of strength

Maximum strength is the maximum force a muscle is capable of exerting in a single maximal voluntary contraction, for example in weightlifting.

Explosive strength (elastic) is the ability to overcome resistance with a high speed of contraction, for example the long jump.

Strength endurance is the ability of a muscle to perform repeated contractions and withstand fatigue, for example in endurance-based events.

Dynamic strength is when a force is applied against a resistance, with movement occurring repeatedly over a period of time. This is the product of strength × speed, also known as power output. It is essential for highly explosive activities, such as sprinting.

Static strength is the ability to apply a force where the length of the muscle does not change and there is no visible movement at a joint, for example a gymnast holding a balance.

Exam tip

Make sure you can give a sporting example of each type of strength.

Factors affecting strength

Strength is dependent on two factors:

- Fibre type (Figure 12) — fast-twitch fibres contract more quickly and produce more power and maximum strength. They are also designed to grow larger as a result of training.
- Cross-sectional area of the muscle — the greater the cross-sectional area, the greater the strength produced. Muscles with the largest cross-sectional area tend to be found in the legs. There is a maximum of 16–30 newtons of force per cm^2 of muscle cross-section.

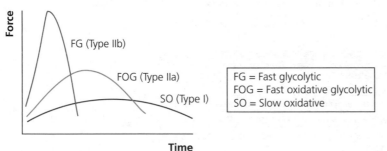

Time

Figure 12 Effect of fibre type on force production

Methods of evaluating each type of strength

Evaluating strength ensures that a training programme is designed correctly. For your exam you need to know the tests shown in Table 16.

Table 16 Methods of evaluating strength

Maximum strength	Hand grip dynamometer	The performer squeezes the dynamometer while lowering it from shoulder height to their side. The highest reading from three attempts is recorded. This is a simple, objective and cheap measure, but only measures the forearm muscles and is not sport specific
	1RM max test	The performer lifts the maximum weight they can just once. This allows most muscle groups to be tested, but it is difficult to isolate individual muscles. It is easy to carry out, but care needs to be taken to avoid injury
Explosive strength	Vertical jump	This measures a standing vertical jump, where data can be converted to calculate power output. Easy to set up but only measures explosive strength in the legs
Strength endurance	UK abdominal curl test	The performer does as many sit-ups as they can in time with a beep. This is a progressive test and finishes when the performer can no longer keep up with the beep and the stage reached is recorded. It is good for large groups, cheap and reliable, and isolates the abdominal muscles. This is a maximal test, so motivation is a factor, and it is not sport specific
	Press-up test	The performer completes as many press-ups as they can until they can no longer continue. The performer needs to be motivated because this is a maximal test but no equipment is required, it is cheap and simple to carry out, and there are normative data available for comparison

Training to develop strength

Improvements in strength result from working against some form of resistance, and it is important to consider the type of strength that needs to be developed (Table 17). To do this the following factors must be considered:

- resistance (in this case the weight as a percentage of one repetition maximum)
- repetitions (number of times the exercise is repeated)
- number of sets (series of repetitions and relief period)
- work–relief ratio (number of work and relief periods, for example 1 : 2 means double the relief time compared with work time)

Table 17 Strength training guidelines for maximum, explosive and endurance

Type of strength	Intensity (% of one rep max)	Repetitions	Sets	Work–relief ratio	Recovery between sets
Maximum	85–95%	1–5	2–6	1:3+	4–5 min
Explosive	75–85%	6–10	4–6	1:3	3–5 min
Endurance (advanced)	50–75%	15–20	3–5	1:2	30–45 s
Endurance (basic)	25–50%	15–20	4–6	1:2	60 s

Weight training

Weight training is usually described in terms of sets and repetitions. The number of sets and repetitions that you do and the amount of weight you lift will depend on the type of strength you wish to improve. Before you can design a programme, it is important to determine the maximum amount of weight that can be lifted with one repetition (1RM). This means that weight training can be flexible, so if maximum strength is the goal, heavy weights need to be lifted with low repetitions, for example three sets of 2–6 repetitions at 80–100% of maximum load. However, if strength endurance is the goal, more repetitions using lighter weights need to be performed, for example 3 sets of 10 repetitions at approximately 50% of maximum load. Weight training increases muscle strength, posture and alignment, but for safety it is important to have a 'spotter' when using heavy weights.

Knowledge check 20

Explain how weight training will be different for an endurance performer compared with a power athlete.

A multi-gym involves a fitness system with different stations designed to perform a wide range of exercises. It involves machines with adjustable weight stacks rather than free weights. Lifting is more controlled and often limits sport-specific movement patterns.

Plyometric training

If explosive strength is crucial to a successful performance, for example in the long jump and 100 m sprint in athletics, then plyometrics is a suitable method of strength training. It involves high-intensity explosive activities, for example hopping and jumping, and works on the concept that muscles can generate more force if they have previously been stretched. An eccentric contraction occurs first followed by a concentric contraction (stretch-shortening cycle). Plyometric training involves three phases:

1 Eccentric phase — on landing, the muscle performs an eccentric contraction, which stretches the muscle.

2 Amortisation phase — the stage between the eccentric and concentric muscle contractions. This time needs to be short so that the energy stored from the eccentric contraction is not lost.

3 Concentric contraction phase — uses the stored energy to increase the force of the contraction.

To develop leg strength a plyometric circuit needs to be high-intensity, with 2–6 repetitions — for example, 4 × 10 m alternate leg hopping, 2 × deep squat jumps for 30 seconds. Full recovery is needed between repetitions and at least 2 rest days in between sessions to avoid injury.

Circuit and interval training

Circuit training involves a series of exercise stations, such as press-ups, sit-ups and squat thrusts. The resistance used is the athlete's body weight, and each exercise concentrates on a different muscle group to allow for recovery. A circuit is usually designed for strength endurance, but can be easily adapted to develop maximum or explosive strength using plyometric exercises or free weights arranged in a circuit. A skill circuit can also be performed to make training more sport specific.

Interval training is similar to circuit training as there is a relief period between each exercise station. When designing interval and circuit training it is important to consider work intensity (how many stations/repetitions), work duration, relief intervals and number of work/relief intervals.

Physiological adaptations from strength training

Regular strength training over a period of at least 12 weeks will result in muscle and connective tissue, metabolic and neural adaptations. It can also produce an improvement in strength of 25–100% within 6 months.

Muscle and connective tissues

The type of strength training you do will result in specific adaptations. With weight training, for example, light weights and high repetitions allow adaptations to occur in slow oxidative fibres, whereas heavy weights and low repetitions allow adaptations in fast glycolytic fibres.

Aerobic adaptations to slow oxidative fibres include:
- hypertrophy of slow-twitch fibres. This is where the myofibrils become thicker due to increased muscle synthesis. However, hypertrophy in slow-twitch muscle fibres is not as pronounced as in fast-twitch fibres
- an increase in mitochondria and myoglobin
- an increase in glycogen and triglyceride stores
- an increase in capillary density

Anaerobic adaptations to fast-twitch fibres include:
- hypertrophy of fast oxidative glycolytic and fast glycolytic fibres
- muscle hyperplasia
- an increase in ATP and PC stores
- an increase in glycogen stores
- greater tolerance of lactic acid

Hyperplasia is the splitting of muscle fibres, leading to the creation of new ones. Together with muscle hypertrophy it contributes to an increase in size of the muscle.

Strength training increases bone density and mass, which improves the absorption of calcium and lowers the risk of osteoporosis. It also increases the strength of tendons and ligaments, helping joint stability and reducing injury.

Neural

More strength can be generated by the recruitment of a greater number of fast-twitch motor units. The inhibitory effect of the Golgi tendon organs is reduced, which allows the muscle to stretch further and generate more force.

Metabolic

ATP, PC and glycogen stores in the muscles increase, which gives increased energy for anaerobic activities. Enzyme activity also increases, which improves the efficiency of anaerobic energy production. An increase in buffering capacity delays OBLA. Finally, an increase in muscle mass results in improved body composition and helps manage body weight through greater energy expenditure.

Hyperplasia When muscle fibres split in order to create new ones.

Knowledge check 21

Identify three metabolic adaptations that result from strength training.

Flexibility training

Types of flexibility

There are two types of flexibility:

- Static flexibility is the range of movement around a joint without reference to speed or movement, for example doing the splits. It can be active, where a joint is pushed beyond its point of resistance, lengthening the muscles and surrounding connective tissue, or passive, when a stretch occurs with the help of an external force, such as a partner, gravity or a wall.
- Dynamic flexibility is the range of movement around a joint with reference to speed and movement. It involves the resistance of a joint to movement, for example when a dancer performs a split leap.

Factors that affect joint stability

- The elasticity of ligaments and tendons — for example, the hip and shoulder are both ball-and-socket joints, but the hip joint has a deeper joint cavity and tighter ligaments to keep it more stable, but less mobile, than the shoulder.
- The amount of stretch allowed by surrounding muscles.
- The type of joint — for example, the knee is a hinge joint allowing movement in only one plane (flexion and extension). The shoulder is a ball-and-socket joint and allows movement in many planes (flexion, extension, abduction, adduction, horizontal flexion and extension, medial and lateral rotation, circumduction).
- Age — the older you are, the less flexible you are due to loss of elasticity in connective tissues.
- Gender — females tend to be more flexible than males due to higher levels of the hormones oestrogen and relaxin.

Exam tip

For your exam you need to know how joint type, nature of surrounding tissue (ligament, tendons and muscles), age and gender can affect flexibility.

Methods of evaluating flexibility

For your exam you need to know about two tests:

- The sit-and-reach test only gives an indication of flexibility of the hamstrings and lower back. Participants sit on the floor with their feet flat against a box and legs straight, then reach forward as far as possible and hold for 2 seconds; the best score is recorded. This is a simple, cheap and easily accessible test with standardised data available to compare results and obtain a rating.
- A goniometer is an instrument that measures angles at various joints. It is an objective, valid and reliable test, but it is quite difficult to locate the axis of rotation.

Exam tip

Flexibility tests are joint specific. So, for example, a high score in the sit-and-reach test only shows that there is good flexibility in the hamstrings and lower back.

Training used to develop flexibility

Static and passive stretching

Static stretching is when the muscle is held in a stationary position for 30 seconds or more. It can be active, where a joint is pushed beyond its point of resistance, lengthening the muscles and surrounding connective tissue, or passive, when a stretch occurs with the help of an external force, such as a partner, gravity or a wall.

Ballistic stretching

Ballistic stretching involves performing a stretch with swinging or bouncing movements to push a body part even further, and is suitable for activities where a large force of contraction is needed. However, it can be dangerous if not performed correctly, and there is a risk of injury if the performer is not very flexible.

Isometric stretching

This begins with a static, passive stretch and then the performer contracts their muscles isometrically for up to 20 seconds, for example pushing against a wall.

Dynamic stretching

This involves controlled leg or arm movements that take a body part gently to the limit of its range of motion, for example a walking lunge.

Proprioceptive neuromuscular facilitation (PNF)

This is where the muscle is contracted isometrically for a period of at least 10 seconds. It is then relaxed and stretched again, usually going much further the second time because the inhibitory signals sent from Golgi tendon organs override the excitatory signals from the muscle spindles, thus delaying the stretch reflex.

As the leg is passively stretched again, the Golgi tendon organs are responsible for the antagonist muscle relaxing, which means the leg stretches further. This process can be repeated until no more gains are possible (Figure 13).

Knowledge check 22

Which types of flexibility training would be most suitable for a gymnast?

Figure 13 PNF in practice: (a) the leg is stretched for at least 10 seconds; (b) the leg is relaxed; (c) the leg is stretched for a second time and stretches further as a result

Physiological adaptations from flexibility training

Adaptations occur after a period of flexibility training 3–6 times per week for 6 weeks.

Muscle and connective tissues

The tendons, ligaments and muscles surrounding a joint have elastic properties, which allow a change in resting length, increasing the range of movement around a joint. There is more of a change to muscle tissue resulting from flexibility training than to tendons or ligaments.

Impact of training on lifestyle diseases

Cardiovascular system

Regular physical activity has a positive effect on **coronary heart disease** because it keeps the heart healthy and more efficient, and increases coronary circulation. **Atherosclerosis** leads to chronic high blood pressure, but exercise prevents hardening and loss of elasticity in arterial walls, lowers bad LDL cholesterol levels and significantly increases good HDL cholesterol levels. This reduces blood fats, slowing the development of atherosclerosis. Exercise also reduces the risk of **heart attack**

Coronary heart disease Occurs when, as a result of atherosclerosis, blood flow and oxygen delivery to the cardiac muscle is reduced, leading to angina or heart attack.

Atherosclerosis A build up of fatty deposits in the arterial walls, which progressively narrows the lumen and hardens the walls.

Heart attack Occurs when a blockage in the coronary artery cuts off blood flow to the cardiac muscle.

because blood viscosity decreases, which reduces the resistance to blood flow and therefore lowers blood pressure by up to 5–10 mmHg. Training also helps you to maintain a healthy weight, which can reduce your risk of **stroke** by up to 27%.

Respiratory system

Regular training maintains full use and elasticity of lung tissue, decreasing the risk of **chronic obstructive pulmonary disease (COPD)**. It also improves the efficiency of the respiratory system, which maximises gaseous exchange due to an increase in the surface area of alveoli and capillary density at the alveoli. Respiratory muscles are strengthened, which alleviates the symptoms of **asthma**. Tidal volume and minute ventilation increase, also allowing greater gaseous exchange.

Summary

After studying this topic you should be able to plan a personal health and fitness programme with knowledge of:
- aerobic capacity and maximal oxygen uptake (VO_2 max), strength (static, dynamic, maximum, explosive and endurance) and flexibility (static and dynamic)
- the affecting factors, evaluation methods, types of training and physiological adaptations for each of these fitness components
- the structure and application of periodisation of training (macrocycle, mesocycle and microcycle)
- the cardiovascular system diseases: coronary heart disease (CHD), stroke, atherosclerosis and heart attack
- the respiratory system diseases: asthma and chronic obstructive pulmonary disease (COPD)

Injury prevention and the rehabilitation of injury

Acute injuries

An **acute injury** is a sudden injury caused by a specific impact or traumatic event, where a sharp pain is felt immediately. For your exam you need to know about hard- and soft-tissue acute injuries and concussion.

Fractures (hard tissue)

A break or a crack in a bone is a fracture. A simple or closed fracture is a clean break to a bone that does not penetrate through the skin or damage any surrounding tissue. A compound or open fracture is when the soft tissue or skin has been damaged. This is more serious because there is a higher risk of infection.

Dislocations (hard tissue)

Dislocation occurs at a joint and is very painful. It happens when the ends of bones are forced out of position.

Strains (soft tissue)

A strain — often called a 'pulled' or 'torn' muscle — occurs when muscle fibres are stretched too far and tear.

Stroke Results from a blockage in the cerebral artery, which cuts off blood supply to the brain (ischaemic stroke) or causes the blood vessel to burst (haemorrhagic stroke).

Chronic obstructive pulmonary disease (COPD) An umbrella term for a variety of lung conditions in which the airways become inflamed and narrow, leading to permanent changes, a reduction in quality of life and an inability to exercise.

Asthma Constriction of bronchial airways and inflammation of the mucous membranes, which limits breathing.

Acute injury An injury where pain is felt immediately during activity.

Sprains (soft tissue)

Sprains occur to ligaments (strong bands of tissue around joints that join bone to bone) when they are stretched too far or tear.

Contusion and haematoma (soft tissue)

A contusion is an area where blood vessels have become damaged. Haematoma is internal bleeding, from minor bruises under the skin to deep tissue bleeding.

Abrasions and blisters (soft tissue)

These are minor injuries. An abrasion is the result of a scrape, and damages the surface of the skin. A blister occurs as a result of friction on the skin.

Concussion

Concussion is a more serious injury and occurs after a blow to the head. It results in dizziness, sickness, nausea and can cause loss of consciousness.

Chronic injuries

Chronic injuries are often referred to as 'overuse' injuries and occur after playing sport or exercise for a long time. For your exam you need to know about hard- and soft-tissue chronic injuries.

Chronic injury An injury that results from overuse.

Achilles tendonitis (soft tissue)

Tendonitis causes pain and inflammation of the tendon. The Achilles tendon is at the back of the ankle and is the largest tendon in the body. It connects the gastrocnemius to the heel bone and is used for walking, running and jumping, so when we do a lot of regular activity it can be prone to tendonitis.

Stress fracture (hard tissue)

Stress fractures are most common in the weight-bearing bones of the legs, often when there is a rapid increase in the amount of exercise or in the intensity of an activity. Muscles become fatigued, so they are no longer able to absorb the added shock of exercise. The fatigued muscle eventually transfers the stress overload to bone and the result is a tiny crack called a stress fracture. The area becomes tender and swollen.

Shin splints (soft tissue)

The tendons that connect the muscles to the tibia via the periosteum become inflamed, resulting in chronic shin pain.

'Tennis elbow' (soft tissue)

Tennis elbow occurs in the muscles attached to the elbow that are used to straighten the wrist. The muscles and tendons become inflamed and tiny tears occur on the outside of the elbow. The area becomes sore and tender. Any activity that places repeated stress on the elbow through overuse of the muscles and tendons of the forearm can cause tennis elbow.

Knowledge check 23

Give one example of
(a) an acute injury and
(b) a chronic injury.

Injury prevention

Intrinsic injury risk factors

These occur where there is an injury risk or force from inside the body. They include:

- individual variables, such as poor body posture and alignment, age, previous injuries and poor nutrition
- training effects, such as poor preparation, inadequate fitness and lack of flexibility

Extrinsic injury risk factors

These occur where there is an injury risk or force from outside the body. They include:

- poor technique and training, which can place excessive stress on muscles, tendons and ligaments
- incorrect equipment and clothing
- inappropriate intensity, duration or frequency of activity — it is important not to overload the body too quickly

The debate surrounding effective warm-up and cool-down

A warm-up help prepares the body for exercise and consists of a pulse raiser, stretching and game-related activities. The benefits of a warm-up are:

- a reduction in the possibility of injury
- an increase in the elasticity of the muscle
- the release of synovial fluid
- an increase in muscle temperature
- better oxygen delivery through increased blood flow to muscle tissues
- increased speed of nerve conduction, which improves reaction time
- an opportunity for rehearsal of movement patterns used in the activity
- mental rehearsal

The physiological benefits of a cool-down are:
- keeping the skeletal muscle pump working
- maintaining venous return
- preventing blood pooling in the veins
- the removal of lactic acid

Recent areas of debate include not using static stretches in a warm-up, with dynamic stretching considered to be more effective because the muscle is then better prepared for sudden dynamic loads. There is also little evidence to suggest that a cool-down can prevent or limit **DOMS**. In addition, evidence has shown that a passive recovery period, such as sitting on a bench, is more beneficial for an aerobically fit athlete than an active cool-down.

Responding to injuries and medical conditions in a sporting environment

Assessing injuries using SALTAPS

SALTAPS is a sport-specific assessment approach for considering whether a player should continue in an activity after an injury:

> ### Knowledge check 24
> What is the difference between an intrinsic risk factor and an extrinsic risk factor?

> **DOMS** Delayed onset of muscle soreness, where pain and stiffness are usually felt around 24 hours after exercise.

> **SALTAPS** The steps needed to assess an injury: see, ask, look, touch, active movement, passive movement and strength testing.

- **S**ee the game in which the player is injured and observe the injury.
- **A**sk questions about the injury — for example, where does it hurt? How did it happen?
- **L**ook at the injury site for bruising, bleeding, swelling or deformity.
- **T**ouch the area gently to feel for swelling, deformity, heat or lumps/bumps.
- **A**ctive movement — check whether the performer can move the injured area.
- **P**assive movement — here the assessor moves the injured body part.
- **S**trength testing — see whether the performer can stand, lift or put pressure on the injured area, and ask whether they feel able to continue.

Acute management of soft-tissue injuries using PRICE

Using **PRICE** can help to minimise a soft-tissue injury by reducing swelling, easing pain and preventing further damage (Figure 14).

Most minor soft tissue injuries can be managed at home. For the first two to three days after your injury, you should follow the PRICE procedure.

PRICE Stands for protect, rest, ice, compress and elevate.

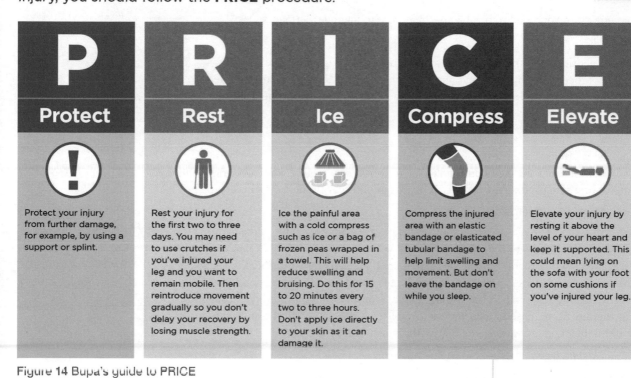

P Protect

Protect your injury from further damage, for example, by using a support or splint.

R Rest

Rest your injury for the first two to three days. You may need to use crutches if you've injured your leg and you want to remain mobile. Then reintroduce movement gradually so you don't delay your recovery by losing muscle strength.

I Ice

Ice the painful area with a cold compress such as ice or a bag of frozen peas wrapped in a towel. This will help reduce swelling and bruising. Do this for 15 to 20 minutes every two to three hours. Don't apply ice directly to your skin as it can damage it.

C Compress

Compress the injured area with an elastic bandage or elasticated tubular bandage to help limit swelling and movement. But don't leave the bandage on while you sleep.

E Elevate

Elevate your injury by resting it above the level of your heart and keep it supported. This could mean lying on the sofa with your foot on some cushions if you've injured your leg.

Figure 14 Bupa's guide to PRICE

Bupa UK, PRICE info graphic, www.bupa.co.uk/health-information, 2016

Recognising concussion using the six Rs

Concussion is a serious brain injury that for some can result in fatality. World Rugby launched a 'recognise and remove' campaign, involving the **six Rs**:

- **R**ecognise the signs and symptoms of concussion.
- **R**emove the player from the field of play immediately.
- **R**efer immediately to a qualified healthcare professional who is trained in evaluating and treating concussion.

Knowledge check 25

What type of injury would PRICE be used for?

Six Rs Recognise, remove, refer, rest, recover and return.

- **R**est the player from exercise until they are symptom-free and ensure they are not left alone for the first 24 hours.
- **R**ecover and be symptom-free for a minimum of 1 week for adults and 2 weeks for under 18s before seeking an authorised return from a healthcare professional.
- **R**eturn when symptom-free with written authorisation and having completed the GRTP (graduated return to play protocol).

Rehabilitation of injury

Rehabilitation involves returning an injury back to full function. There are three recognised stages of rehabilitation: the early stage, where gentle exercise encourages the damaged tissue to heal; the mid stage, involving progressive loading to the injury site; and the late stage, where functional exercises take place to ensure the injured site is ready for action.

Treatments

For your exam you need to be able to explain the following treatments.

Stretching

At first, gentle static and passive stretching exercises are used to speed up the recovery process. As swelling and bleeding subside, PNF stretches can be added to retrain the stretch reflex. Finally, active and dynamic stretches can be used to further strengthen and increase the range of mobility.

Massage

Massage is effective for most soft-tissue injuries. It improves circulation, moving fluid and nutrients through damaged tissue to encourage healing, and accelerates the removal of waste products. Elasticity is improved and scar tissue is broken down.

Heat-and-cold contrast therapy

Cryotherapy is the use of a cold temperature to treat injuries. The ice has an analgesic effect and can limit pain and swelling by causing vasoconstriction of blood vessels, decreasing blood flow to the injured area. Heat therapy uses heat to reduce muscle tension, stiffness and pain. It vasodilates blood vessels, increasing blood flow and the healing response in the damaged area. Contrast therapy alternates cold and heat therapy to increase blood flow and decrease swelling/pain after exercise, but should only take place several days after the injury has occurred.

Cryotherapy The use of very low temperatures to treat a variety of injuries.

Anti-inflammatory drugs

Non-steroid anti-inflammatory drugs (NSAIDs) are taken to reduce inflammation, temperature and pain following injury.

Physiotherapy

Physiotherapy involves physical treatment performed by a trained medical expert, using methods such as mobilisation, massage, exercise therapy and postural training.

Surgery

There are two types of surgery. In arthroscopy (keyhole surgery), which is carried out under general or local anaesthetic, a small incision is made and a tiny camera with associated surgical tools is inserted to guide and repair the injury. This minimises damage to surrounding tissues, resulting in less pain and reduced risk of infection, as well as a faster initial recovery time. In open surgery, which is carried out under general or local anaesthetic, an incision is made to open a joint in order to repair or reconstruct any damage. This can create a stronger repair, but the risk of infection is higher and scarring is significant.

Treatment of common sporting injuries

For your exam you need to describe how to treat fractures, joint injuries and exercise-induced muscle damage.

Simple fracture and dislocation

A simple fracture needs medical attention but until this happens it is important to keep the patient comfortable, calm and still. For a dislocation, only a medical professional should try to reposition bones. At hospital the injury will be immobilised with a plaster cast, sling or crutches and, if necessary, surgery used to realign or pin bones. Anti-inflammatory and pain relief medication (NSAIDs) may also be prescribed. Physiotherapy could be needed to improve mobility and strengthen the surrounding connective tissue.

Stress fracture

A stress fracture is usually diagnosed by a medical expert, followed by ice treatment to reduce swelling. It is important to rest this injury for up to 6 weeks (this could be longer, depending on severity). Immobilisation with a splint or brace may be necessary, and anti-inflammatory and pain relief medication may be prescribed. Return to exercise is gentle at first, consisting of strengthening exercises for the surrounding connective tissue.

Sprain

For a sprain, follow PRICE. In first few days the injury should be rested, but after this (depending on the severity) it is important to try to keep moving so that the joint does not become stiff. NSAIDs can be taken, alongside strengthening exercises for the surrounding connective tissue. Severe sprains might require surgery.

Torn cartilage

With torn cartilage, medical attention will be required. PRICE should be followed and NSAIDs taken to reduce pain and inflammation. Most cartilage injuries require support through a brace or strapping, and in some cases arthroscopic surgery can be used correct the damage.

Exercise-induced muscle damage

Microscopic injuries to muscle fibres do not usually require medical attention and symptoms should improve within 5 days. Treatment should include the use of ice, NSAIDs, massage and stretching techniques.

Exam tip

Make sure that you can give an injury example for each of these treatment methods.

Knowledge check 26

Explain the importance of cold therapy in the rehabilitation of an injury.

Summary

After studying this topic you should be able to:

- describe acute hard- and soft-tissue injuries, concussion and chronic hard- and soft-tissue injuries
- explain the intrinsic and extrinsic risk factors to consider in injury prevention
- identify the effectiveness of a warm–up and a cool–down
- understand injury assessment using SALTAPS and acute injury management using PRICE
- recognise concussion and follow the six Rs
- explain the following treatment methods used in injury rehabilitation: stretching, massage, heat-and-cold contrast therapy, anti-inflammatory drugs, physiotherapy and surgery
- outline the treatments for fractures, joint injuries and exercise-induced muscle damage

■ Biomechanics

Biomechanical principles, levers and the use of technology

Newton's laws of motion

Newton's first law of inertia states that 'every body continues in its state of rest or motion in a straight line, unless compelled to change that state by external forces exerted upon it'. In a penalty situation, the ball (body) will remain on the spot (state of rest) unless it is kicked by the player (an external force is exerted upon it).

Newton's second law of acceleration states that 'the rate of momentum of a body (or the acceleration for a body of constant mass) is proportional to the force causing it and the change that takes place in the direction in which the force acts': force = mass × acceleration ($F = ma$). When the player kicks (force) the ball during the game, the acceleration of the ball (rate of change of momentum) is proportional to the size of the force. So, the harder the ball is kicked, the further and faster it will go.

Newton's third law of action/reaction states that 'to every action force there is an equal and opposite reaction force'. When a footballer jumps up (action) to win a header, a force is exerted on the ground in order to gain height. At the same time, the ground exerts an upward force (equal and opposite reaction) on the player.

Forces

For your exam you need to know about the external **forces** of weight, reaction, air resistance and friction.

Weight

Weight is a gravitational force that the Earth exerts on a body, pulling it towards the centre of the Earth or, effectively, downwards. It is measured in newtons (N).

Reaction

A reaction occurs when two bodies are in contact with one another. It is the equal and opposite force exerted by a body in response to an action force.

Friction

Static **friction** occurs before an object starts to slide, while sliding friction acts between two surfaces that are moving relative to one another. Friction can be affected by the following factors:

- The surface characteristics of the two bodies in contact. Think of a 100 m sprinter who wears running spikes. These help to increase friction because the spikes make contact with the track and therefore maximise acceleration.
- The temperature of the two surfaces in contact. In curling, for example, the ice is swept in front of the curling stone. The sweeping action slightly raises the surface temperature of the ice, reducing the friction between the stone and the ice, and allowing the stone to travel further.
- The mass of the object that is sliding. A larger mass results in greater friction.

Newton's first law of inertia A force is required to change the state of motion.

Newton's second law of acceleration The magnitude (size) and direction of the force determine the magnitude and direction of the acceleration.

Newton's third law of action/reaction For every action force there is an equal and opposite reaction force.

Exam tip

Make sure that you can identify and give a sporting example for each law of motion, because an exam question may refer to a specific law. For example, 'Using Newton's first law of motion...'

Force Something which changes a body's state of motion.

Friction Occurs when two or more bodies are in contact with one another.

Air resistance

Air resistance opposes the motion of a body travelling through the air and depends on:

- The velocity of the moving body — the greater the velocity, the more air resistance.
- The cross-sectional area of the moving body — for example, a cyclist crouches low over the handlebars to reduce cross-sectional area and air resistance.
- The shape and the surface characteristics of a moving body — for example, Lycra suits or aerofoil-shaped helmets make the performer more streamlined.

How forces act on the performer during linear motion

Forces are vectors. How they act on a performer can be shown using arrows on a free body diagram. The position, direction and length of each arrow are important and need to be drawn accurately. The length of the arrow drawn reflects the magnitude or size of the force. The longer the arrow, the bigger the size of the force. When the **net force** is 0 there is no change in the state of motion and so this is a **balanced force**. An **unbalanced force** results in a change in the state of motion.

Exam tip

Friction and air resistance act on the horizontal component and reaction and weight on the vertical component.

Net force The resultant force acting on a body when all other forces have been considered.

Balanced force When forces acting on a body are equal in size but opposite in direction.

Unbalanced force When a force acting in one direction on a body is larger than a force acting in the opposite direction.

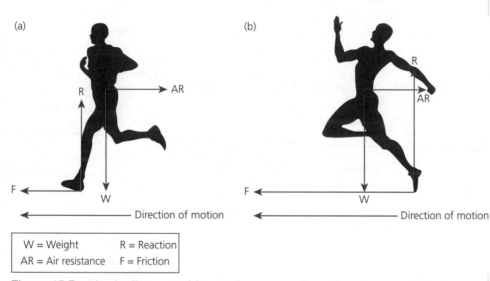

| W = Weight | R = Reaction |
| AR = Air resistance | F = Friction |

Figure 15 Free body diagrams: (a) marathon runner travelling at a constant velocity ($W = R$, $F = AR$) has balanced forces, so net force = 0; (b) long jumper accelerating forwards and upwards at take-off ($R > W$, $F > AR$) has unbalanced forces with a positive net force, so the long jumper experiences forward and vertical acceleration

Calculations of force, momentum, acceleration and weight

For your exam you need to know how to calculate force, weight, acceleration and momentum (Table 18).

Knowledge check 27

Identify and explain two external forces acting on a sprinter.

Table 18 Summary of the required formulas for key biomechanical terms

Measurements of linear motion	Definition	Unit of measurement	How to calculate (if relevant)
Force	A push or pull that alters the state of motion of a body	Newtons (N)	mass (kg) × acceleration (m/s^2)
Weight	The gravitational force exerted on an object	Newtons (N)	weight (N) = mass (kg) × gravitational field strength (N/kg)
Acceleration	The rate of change of velocity	Metres per second squared (m/s^2)	$\dfrac{\text{change in velocity (m/s)}}{\text{time (s)}}$
Momentum	The product of the mass and velocity of an object	Kilogram metres per second (kg m/s)	momentum (kg m/s) = mass (kg) × velocity (m/s)

Centre of mass

Centre of mass is the point of balance of a body. The human body is an irregular shape, so the centre of mass cannot be identified easily. In addition, the body is constantly moving, so the centre of mass will change as a result. In general, the centre of mass for someone adopting a standing position is in the region between the hips and differs according to gender. Males have more weight concentrated in their shoulders and upper body, so their centre of mass is slightly higher than in females, who have more body weight concentrated at their hips. If an athlete raises their arms, their centre of mass will move up. The centre of mass can also be outside the body and act as a point of rotation.

When performing the Fosbury flop in the high jump, the centre of mass of the performer passes under the bar, while their body goes over. This technique is beneficial because the high jumper does not have to lift their centre of mass by as great a distance in order to clear the bar.

In the 'set' position of a sprint start, an athlete moves their centre of mass towards the edge of their base of support to create momentum. As they move when they hear the starting pistol, they lift their hands off the track and become off balance as the line of gravity falls in front of the support base. This allows the athlete to fall forward, creating the speed they require to drive forwards from the blocks.

Factors affecting stability

Stability is affected by:

- The height of the centre of mass — lowering the centre of mass increases stability.
- The position of the line of gravity — this should be central over the base of support to increase stability.
- The area of the support base — the more contact points, the larger the base of support becomes and the more stable the body becomes; for example, a headstand has more contact points than a handstand, so is a more balanced position.
- The mass of the performer — often, the greater the mass, the more stability there is because of increased inertia.

Centre of mass The point of balance of a body.

Knowledge check 28

How can a rugby player increase their stability as they are about to tackle an opponent?

Levers

There are three classes of lever: first, second and third. The classification of each depends on the positions of the fulcrum, load and effort in relation to each other.

First-class lever

Here the fulcrum lies between the effort and the load. There are two examples of this type of lever in the body: the movement of the head and neck during flexion and extension, and extension of the elbow.

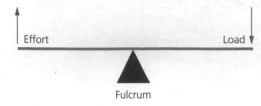

Figure 16 First-class lever

Second-class lever

In second-class levers load lies between the fulcrum and the effort. There is only one example of this type of lever in the body: plantarflexion of the ankle.

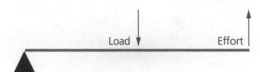

Figure 17 Second-class lever

Third-class lever

Third-class levers can be found in all the other joints of the body, where the effort lies between the fulcrum and the load.

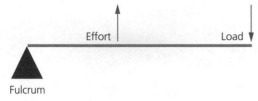

Figure 18 Third-class lever

Mechanical advantage of a second-class lever

A second-class lever has a **mechanical advantage** due to the lengths of the force arm and the load arm. The force arm is the name given to the shortest perpendicular distance between the fulcrum and the application of force (effort). The load arm is the shortest perpendicular distance between the fulcrum and the load (Figure 19). In a second-class lever the force arm is longer than the load arm. This means that the lever system can move a large load over a short distance and requires little effort — for example, lifting one's whole body weight when the foot plantarflexes.

Exam tip

Remember the rhyming mnemonic 'FLE 123', where 123 is the type of lever and FLE refers to the component that is in the middle. So, for example, 'F' for fulcrum is the first letter, so when the fulcrum is in the middle it is a first class lever.

Mechanical advantage Occurs when the force arm is longer than the load arm.

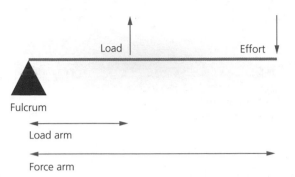

Figure 19 The load arm and the force arm

Analysing movement through the use of technology

For your exam you need to be able to understand and define the use of limb kinematics, force plates and wind tunnels, and explain how they optimise performance (Table 19).

Table 19 The use of technology to analyse movement

Type of technology	Definition	Use	How it helps optimise performance
Limb kinematics	Imaging the position, angle, velocity and acceleration of body segments and joints during motion	Using computer software, this allows for analysis of motion and of joint and limb efficiency	Data can be used to make adjustments in technique to improve performance
Force plates	A rectangular metal plate is used to measure the size of ground reaction forces	This is used to assess the size and direction of forces acting on the performer, acceleration rates, work and power output	It can be used to improve posture during running and balance, and also to help in rehabilitation
Wind tunnels	This is a steel frame that houses fans within it to produce artificial wind	Instruments in the wind tunnel measure the forces produced by the air against a body's surface	The testing of aerodynamic efficiency improves streamlining

Summary

After studying this topic you should be able to:
- define and apply Newton's laws of motion
- explain net force, and balanced and unbalanced forces
- understand the forces of weight, reaction, friction and air resistance, and draw these forces on free body diagrams with resultant motions
- calculate force, momentum, acceleration and weight
- define centre of mass and explain the factors that affect it
- identify the relationship between centre of mass and stability
- understand the components of first-, second- and third-class lever systems, and explain the mechanical advantage of a second-class lever
- define and describe the use of limb kinematics, force plates and wind tunnels, and explain how they can optimise performance

Linear motion, angular motion, fluid mechanics and projectile motion

Linear motion

Linear motion is motion in a straight or curved line, with all body parts moving the same distance at the same speed in the same direction. It occurs when there is a direct force through the centre of mass.

Definitions, calculations and units of measurement

For your exam you need to be able to define, calculate and give units of measurement for each of the quantities of linear motion in Table 20.

Table 20 Definitions, calculations and units of measurement for distance, speed, displacement, velocity and acceleration

Measurements of linear motion	Definition	Unit of measurement	How to calculate
Distance	The path a body takes as it moves from the starting to the finishing position	Metres (m)	Measured
Speed	A measurement of the body's movement per unit of time with no reference to direction	Metres per second (m/s)	$\dfrac{\text{distance covered (m)}}{\text{time taken (s)}}$
Displacement	The shortest route in a straight line between the starting and finishing positions	Metres (m)	Measured
Velocity	The rate of change of displacement	Metres per second (m/s)	$\dfrac{\text{displacement (m)}}{\text{time taken (s)}}$
Acceleration	The rate of change of velocity	Metres per second squared (m/s²)	$\dfrac{\text{change in velocity (m/s)}}{\text{time (s)}}$

Graphs of linear motion

In your exam you need to be able to plot, label and interpret biomechanical graphs and diagrams.

Distance-time graphs

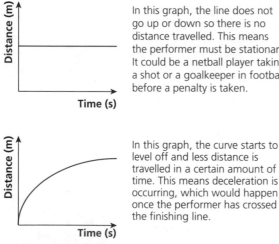

In this graph, the line does not go up or down so there is no distance travelled. This means the performer must be stationary. It could be a netball player taking a shot or a goalkeeper in football before a penalty is taken.

In this graph, the line goes up in a constant diagonal direction. This indicates the distance run is changing at a constant rate and at the same speed. This could occur in the middle of a long-distance race.

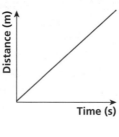

In this graph, the curve starts to level off and less distance is travelled in a certain amount of time. This means deceleration is occurring, which would happen once the performer has crossed the finishing line.

Now the line is curved and gradually gets steeper. This indicates that more distance is being covered in a certain amount of time, so the performer must be accelerating, for example, the first 20 m at the start of a 100 m race.

Figure 20 Distance-time graphs, showing the distance travelled over a period of time

Velocity-time graphs and speed-time graphs

These are essentially the same type of graph. The shape of the velocity-time graph will represent the same pattern of motion as the shape of a speed-time graph. These graphs indicate the velocity or speed of a performer or object per unit of time. The gradient of a graph will help you decide whether a performer is travelling at a constant velocity, accelerating or decelerating.

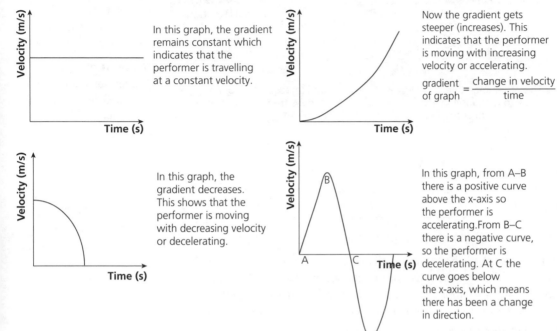

In this graph, the gradient remains constant which indicates that the performer is travelling at a constant velocity.

Now the gradient gets steeper (increases). This indicates that the performer is moving with increasing velocity or accelerating.

$$\text{gradient of graph} = \frac{\text{change in velocity}}{\text{time}}$$

In this graph, the gradient decreases. This shows that the performer is moving with decreasing velocity or decelerating.

In this graph, from A–B there is a positive curve above the x-axis so the performer is accelerating. From B–C there is a negative curve, so the performer is decelerating. At C the curve goes below the x-axis, which means there has been a change in direction.

Figure 21 Velocity-time graphs, showing constant velocity, increasing velocity, decreasing velocity and a more complex pattern of motion

Angular motion

Angular motion is movement around a fixed point or axis, such as a somersault, throwing a discus or moving around the high bar in gymnastics. When angular motion takes place, the body can rotate in one of three axes of rotation (Figure 22).

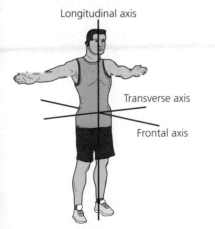

Longitudinal axis

Transverse axis

Frontal axis

Figure 22 The principal axes of rotation

Exam tip

For graphs of linear motion always:

- plot time on the horizontal axis
- label the axes, including units in brackets
- use a curved line of best fit

Angular motion Occurs when a force is applied outside the centre of mass (eccentric force).

For your exam you need to define, calculate and give units of measurement for the quantities of angular motion in Table 21.

Table 21 Definitions, calculations and units of measurement for angular momentum, angular velocity and moment of inertia

Quantity of angular motion	Definition	Unit of measurement	How to calculate
Angular momentum	The quantity of angular motion possessed by a body	$kg\,m^2\,rad/s$	moment of inertia (I) × angular velocity (ω)
Angular velocity	The rate of change in angular displacement	rad/s	$\dfrac{\text{angular displacement}}{\text{time (s)}}$
Moment of inertia	The resistance of a body to a change in its state of angular motion	$kg\,m^2$	Sum (mass × distribution of mass from the axis of rotation^2)

Angular momentum
The quantity of angular motion possessed by a body.

Angular velocity Refers to the speed and direction of spin and is the rate of change in angular displacement.

Moment of inertia
The resistance of a body to change in its state of angular motion or rotation.

Exam tip

Learn the formulas in case you need to do a calculation in your exam, and always show your full workings and the units of measurement to gain some credit even if the final calculation is incorrect.

Factors affecting the size of the moment of inertia of a rotating body

This depends on the mass of the body and the distribution of mass around the axis. The greater the mass, the greater the resistance to change and therefore the greater the moment of inertia — for example, a medicine ball is more difficult to roll along the ground than a basketball. The closer the mass is to the axis of rotation, the easier it is to turn (it has a low moment of inertia). Increasing the distance of the distribution of mass from the axis of rotation increases the moment of inertia, for example, a somersault in a straight position has a higher moment of inertia than a tucked somersault.

Conservation of angular momentum during flight

Angular momentum is a conserved quantity and stays constant unless an external **torque** acts upon it (**angular analogue of Newton's first law of motion**). For example, an ice skater spinning in the air will continue to spin until they land. Here the ground exerts an external force (torque), which changes their state of angular momentum. A figure-skater can also manipulate their moment of inertia to increase or decrease the speed of the spin (angular velocity). At the start of the spin the arms and leg are stretched out (Figure 23). This increases their distance from the axis of rotation, resulting in a large moment of inertia and a large angular momentum in order to start the spin (decrease in angular velocity). When the figure-skater brings his arms and legs back in line with the rest of his body, the distance of these body parts to the axis of rotation decreases significantly (Figure 24). This reduces the moment of inertia, meaning that angular momentum has to increase. The result is a faster spin (increase in angular velocity).

Torque A rotational force.

Angular analogue of Newton's first law of motion States that a rotating body will continue in its state of angular motion unless an external force (torque) is exerted upon it.

Exam tip

Moment of inertia and angular velocity are inversely proportional. When one is high the other is low, and vice versa.

Knowledge check 30

Explain the relationship between moment of inertia and angular velocity.

Figure 23 The start of a spin

Figure 24 Increasing angular velocity during a spin

Graphs of angular velocity, moment of inertia and angular momentum

In Figure 25, the straight body position distributes the diver's mass away from the transverse axis, so his moment of inertia is high and angular velocity is low. In the tucked position the diver's mass moves closer to the transverse axis, so moment of inertia is low and angular velocity is high.

Knowledge check 31

Why do you think the diver wants to increase his moment of inertia prior to entry into the water?

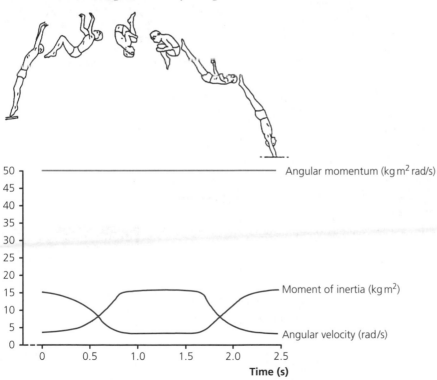

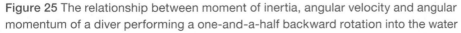

Figure 25 The relationship between moment of inertia, angular velocity and angular momentum of a diver performing a one-and-a-half backward rotation into the water

Fluid mechanics

Drag in water, air resistance on land and lift are dynamic fluid forces. These three forces have an effect on a variety of sports, such as cycling, sprinting and swimming. Any projectile, such as a discus, will also experience drag and lift forces.

Factors that impact on the magnitude of air resistance or drag

- The greater the velocity of a body through a fluid, the greater the air resistance or drag force. Consequently, in a sport that is quick, it is important to reduce the effects of air resistance or drag. This is done by **streamlining** and reducing cross-sectional area.
- Mass — a projectile with a high mass, such as a shot put, travels at a slower velocity, reducing air resistance.
- A large cross-sectional area increases air resistance or drag. In cycling, competitors reduce their cross-sectional area by crouching low over the handlebars, rather than sitting upright.
- A more streamlined, aerodynamic shape reduces air resistance or drag. In cycling, clothing with ridges and an aerodynamic helmet with air ducts have recently been designed to increase streamlining. A swimmer aims to create the narrowest and straightest form as they move through the water.
- Making surface characteristics smooth will reduce air resistance or drag. In swimming and cycling, for example, performers wear special clothing to create a smooth surface and reduce friction between the fluid and body surface.

Streamlining Shaping a body so it can move effectively and quickly through a fluid.

Exam tip

Make sure that you can apply these impact factors to sport by giving examples.

Projectile motion

Projectile motion refers to the movement of either an object or the human body as it travels through the air.

Factors affecting the horizontal distance travelled by a projectile

- **Angle of release** — the optimum angle of release is dependent on release height and landing height. When both the release height and the landing height are equal, for example with a chest pass in basketball, then the optimum angle of release is 45° (ignoring wind resistance and gravity). If the release height is below the landing height, for example shooting in basketball (if we assume the ring is the landing height), then the optimum angle of release needs to be greater than 45°. When the release height is greater than the landing height, for example in the shot put, the optimum angle of release needs to be less than 45°.
- **Speed of release** — the greater the release velocity of a projectile, the greater the horizontal distance travelled.
- **Height of release** — a greater release height also results in an increase in horizontal distance. The force of gravity is constantly acting on the mass of a projectile. This therefore means that, technically, a projectile such as a shot put should be released at the highest point possible above the ground to gain maximum horizontal distance.

Knowledge check 32

Which three factors will affect the horizontal distance of a throw from the boundary line in cricket?

Forces acting on a projectile

Weight (gravity) and air resistance are two forces that affect projectiles while they are in the air. These two factors are crucial in deciding whether a projectile has a flight path that is a true **parabola** or a distorted parabola.

The forces acting on a projectile in flight can be represented with a free body diagram that shows which forces are acting, where the forces originate, the relative sizes of the forces and the direction in which they are acting on the projectile. This enables us to consider the net force acting on the body and therefore the resulting projectile motion and flight path.

Shot put

Projectiles with a large weight force, such as a shot put, have a small air resistance force and follow a true parabolic flight path.

Figure 26 shows the forces affecting the flight path of a shot put at the start, middle and end of flight. As the shot has a large mass there is a longer weight arrow. The longer the flight path, the longer that air resistance can affect a projectile and the greater its influence.

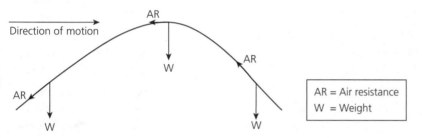

Figure 26 Free body diagram of a shot put in the start-, middle- and end-of-flight phases

Badminton shuttle

In projectiles with a lighter mass, such as a shuttlecock, the effects of air resistance result in a flight path that deviates from a true parabola to create a distorted parabola (Figure 27).

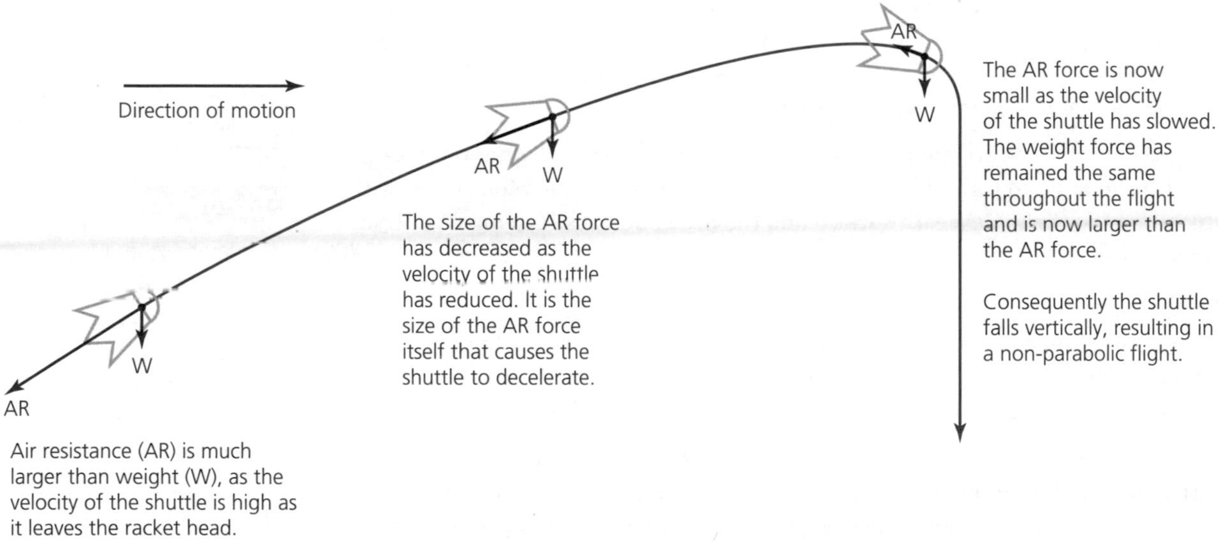

Direction of motion

AR   W

The size of the AR force has decreased as the velocity of the shuttle has reduced. It is the size of the AR force itself that causes the shuttle to decelerate.

W

AR

Air resistance (AR) is much larger than weight (W), as the velocity of the shuttle is high as it leaves the racket head.

AR

W

The AR force is now small as the velocity of the shuttle has slowed. The weight force has remained the same throughout the flight and is now larger than the AR force.

Consequently the shuttle falls vertically, resulting in a non-parabolic flight.

Figure 27 Free body diagram of a shuttle in the start-, mid- and end-of-flight phases

Parabola A uniform curve that is symmetrical at its highest point (i.e. matching left and right sides).

Exam tip

Make sure you draw the release point of the shot put higher than the landing height.

Parallelogram of forces

A parallelogram of forces shows the result of all forces acting on a projectile in flight (Figures 28 and 29).

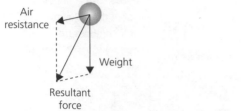

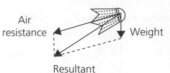

The resultant force shows deceleration to be occurring and weight to be dominant, leading to a parabolic flight path.

Figure 28 Parallelogram of forces for a shot put in mid-flight, showing the resultant force

The resultant force shows deceleration to be occurring and air resistance to be dominant, leading to a non-parabolic flight path.

Figure 29 Parallelogram of forces for a badminton shuttle in mid-flight, showing the resultant force

The Bernoulli principle applied to sporting situations

For your exam you need to be able to explain the **Bernoulli principle** in relation to an upward lift force for the discus, javelin and ski-jumper and a downward lift force for a Formula 1 racing car and track cyclist.

Upward lift force

When the discus is thrown it experiences an upward lift force during flight, which enables the discus to stay in the air for longer and therefore increases the horizontal distance it travels. Lift is achieved when different air pressures act on an object. Air that travels faster has a lower pressure than air that travels slower. This is the Bernoulli principle. When a projectile such as the discus is released the **angle of attack** is important. The angle of attack changes the flow of air around the discus, so the air that travels under the discus has to travel a shorter distance than the air above. This results in the air below the discus travelling at a slower velocity, which therefore creates a higher pressure. This higher pressure below the discus creates an upward lift force and allows the discus to travel further. If the angle of attack is too large, then there is less lift and drag increases, causing the discus to stall.

The angle of attack is also important for a ski-jumper, to create a higher pressure underneath in order to travel further. The ski-jumper adopts an aerofoil shape, with flat skis forming the underneath surface and the head and back forming the curved upper surface.

Downward lift force

The Bernoulli principle can also be used to describe a downward lift force, such as that required by Formula 1 racing cars and track cyclists. The car and bike need to be pushed down into the ground so that a greater frictional force is created.

In Formula 1, the car's rear wing is angled so the lift force can act in a downward direction to push the car into the track. This happens because the air that travels over the top of the car travels a shorter distance than the air underneath due to the angle of the wing. As a result, the air above the car travels at a slower velocity and a higher

Bernoulli principle
Air molecules exert less pressure when they travel faster and more pressure when they travel slower.

Angle of attack The tilt of a projectile relative to the airflow. The optimum angle of attack that produces the best lift for the discus is 25–40°.

Knowledge check 33

Explain the Bernoulli principle in relation to an upward lift force for the javelin.

Exam tip

Remember that the discus, javelin and ski-jumper have an upward lift force to increase how far they travel, while the Formula 1 racing car and track cyclist need a downward lift force to maximise friction and therefore increase speed.

pressure. This creates a downward lift force and therefore a greater frictional force, so the tyres maintain a firm grip on the track as it travels at high speed and around corners.

In cycling, the low streamlined body position over the handlebars together with the shape of the cyclist's helmet creates a flat surface, so the airflow over the top of the cyclist travels a shorter distance at a slower velocity than the air underneath. This results in a higher pressure above the cyclist, creating a downward lift force that increases friction, allowing the tyres of the bike to maintain a firm grip on the track.

Use of spin to create a Magnus force

Spin is created by applying an eccentric force and the consequent **Magnus force** causes deviations to expected flight paths. In golf it can be used to control the landing of a ball, in tennis it is used to outwit an opponent and in football it is used to bend a free kick around a wall of defenders.

When top-spin is applied to a ball, the surface at the top of the ball is travelling in the opposite direction from airflow. This means the air slows down and a high pressure is created. At the bottom of the ball the surface is travelling in the same direction as the airflow so the air accelerates and a lower pressure is created. The result of this difference in pressure between the top and the bottom surface causes the ball to move towards the area of low pressure (bottom surface). This means the ball dips and the distance travelled decreases.

> **Magnus force** The force created from a pressure gradient on opposing surfaces of a spinning projectile.

Low velocity airflow/high pressure area

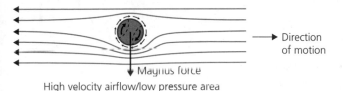

Direction of motion

Magnus force

High velocity airflow/low pressure area

Figure 30 Airflow diagram illustrating the downward Magnus force created by top-spin

With back-spin the surface at the top of the ball is travelling in the same direction as airflow. This means the air accelerates and the pressure drops. The surface at the bottom of the ball now travels in the opposite direction from airflow, so the air slows down and pressure increases. This means that the ball moves towards the area of low pressure, which is now at the top of the ball, resulting in the ball 'floating' and the distance travelled increasing.

Top-spin, side-spin and back-spin in tennis and table tennis

Top-spin rotation occurs when an eccentric force is applied above the centre of mass of a ball. It creates a downwards Magnus force, causing the ball to rotate forwards and resulting in it dipping and travelling a shorter distance. However, when the ball hits the ground it bounces forwards quickly at a low angle to the ground. This increase in speed is used to try to beat an opponent.

Back-spin rotation occurs when an eccentric force is applied underneath the centre of mass. It creates an upwards Magnus force and causes the ball to rotate backwards, resulting in it 'floating' and travelling further in the air. When the ball lands, it bounces up at a large angle from the ground, its speed decreases and it stops quickly or even travels backwards. Back-spin is often used in tennis for a dropshot.

Side-spin rotation creates a Magnus force to the left or right. Whether a ball goes to the left or the right depends on the position of application of the eccentric force. As the ball lands it then leaves the ground in the opposite direction from the spin.

Side-spin in football and hook and slice in golf

Side-spin is used in football and golf to curve the flight of the ball (Table 22).

Table 22 The effect of different types of side-spin on the airflow and flight path of a projectile

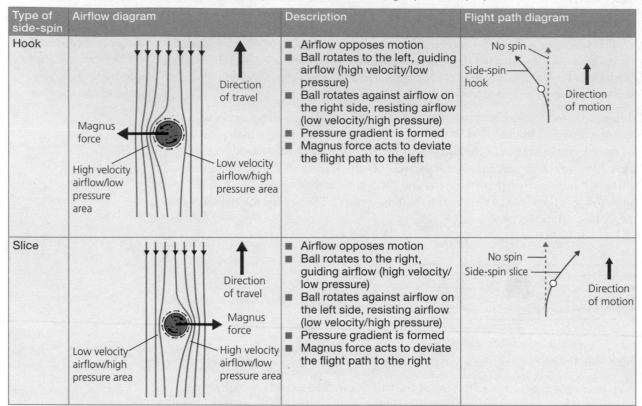

Type of side-spin	Airflow diagram	Description	Flight path diagram
Hook	Direction of travel; Magnus force; High velocity airflow/low pressure area; Low velocity airflow/high pressure area	■ Airflow opposes motion ■ Ball rotates to the left, guiding airflow (high velocity/low pressure) ■ Ball rotates against airflow on the right side, resisting airflow (low velocity/high pressure) ■ Pressure gradient is formed ■ Magnus force acts to deviate the flight path to the left	No spin; Side-spin hook; Direction of motion
Slice	Direction of travel; Magnus force; Low velocity airflow/high pressure area; High velocity airflow/low pressure area	■ Airflow opposes motion ■ Ball rotates to the right, guiding airflow (high velocity/low pressure) ■ Ball rotates against airflow on the left side, resisting airflow (low velocity/high pressure) ■ Pressure gradient is formed ■ Magnus force acts to deviate the flight path to the right	No spin; Side-spin slice; Direction of motion

Summary

After studying this topic you should be able to:
■ understand linear motion and give definitions, calculations and units of measurement for distance, displacement, speed, velocity and acceleration
■ plot and interpet graphs of linear motion
■ understand angular motion and the three axes of rotation
■ define, calculate, give units of measurement and interpret graphs for moment of inertia, angular velocity and angular momentum
■ explain the factors that affect the size of moment of inertia of a rotating body
■ give the relationship between moment of inertia and angular velocity
■ understand the conservation of moment of inertia in relation to Newton's first law of motion
■ explain the factors that affect air resistance and drag

- describe the factors that affect the horizontal distance travelled by a projectile
- draw free body diagrams and the resultant forces acting on a projectile in flight
- draw a parallelogram of forces and identify parabolic and non-parabolic flight paths
- explain, using the Bernoulli principle, how an upward lift force is created for the discus, javelin and shot put
- explain how a downward lift force is created for Formula 1 racing cars and track cyclists
- explain the use of top-spin, side-spin and back-spin to create a Magnus force as well as the use of hook and slice in golf

Questions & Answers

About this section

This section explains the structure of OCR A-level Paper H555/01, and discusses strategies for approaching the different types of question you will encounter. This is followed by a series of sample questions covering all the question types — multiple choice, short answer and extended writing. Each question is followed by a sample student answer, with accompanying comments. You should practise all the questions yourself and compare your answers with the sample student answers. Be sure to read the comments on the answers to improve your understanding of what is required to achieve full marks.

Exam format

Paper 1 is a 2-hour paper, worth 90 marks, and makes up 30% of your A-level. It examines component 01, which includes three topics from the specification:

- Applied anatomy and physiology
- Exercise physiology
- Biomechanics

You will be assessed on a mixture of questions requiring objective, short, medium and extended responses. The paper may also include some multiple-choice questions. It is divided into three sections. Section A is worth 10 marks and consists of five brief 2-mark questions. Section B is worth 60 marks with a mix of questions ranging from 1–6 marks. Finally, section C is worth 20 marks and contains one extended-response question that requires you to draw together knowledge from more than one topic within the component and demonstrate your understanding of how the topics interrelate. You therefore need to link between the topics where possible — if you do not do this, you may not be able to access the top marks. These questions assess AO1, AO2 and AO3:

Assessment objective 1 (AO1)	Here you need to demonstrate your *knowledge* and *understanding* of the factors that underpin performance and involvement in physical activity and sport
Assessment objective 2 (AO2)	This is where you are awarded marks for *applying* your knowledge and understanding of the factors that underpin performance and involvement in physical activity and sport
Assessment objective 3 (AO3)	To gain marks here you need to *analyse* and *evaluate* the factors that underpin performance and involvement in physical activity and sport

The following table shows the weightings of each of these assessment objectives in terms of the overall A-level:

	AO1	AO2	AO3
Paper 1 weightings	12%	12%	6.66%
Overall weightings	25%	25%	20%

This means that on your paper there are more marks available for knowledge and understanding and for application than for analysis and evaluation.

(In the sample answers to extended-response questions in this section, each assessment objective has been labelled (AO1, AO2 and AO3), so it is easier for you to see where the answer demonstrates knowledge and understanding, application and analysis/evaluation.)

Finally, in the exam it is important that you write clearly in the spaces provided in the answer booklet. Avoid writing anything that you want to be marked in the margins, and always indicate if you run out of space that your answer continues on additional paper or at the end of the answer booklet if there is space.

Comments

Each question is followed by a brief analysis of what to watch out for when answering the question. All student responses are then accompanied by comments indicating where credit is due. In the weaker answers, they also point out areas for improvement, specific problems and common errors, such as lack of clarity, weak or non-existent development, irrelevance, misinterpretation of the question and mistaken meanings of terms.

■Applied anatomy and physiology

Skeletal and muscular systems

Question 1

Complete the table below to analyse the position of the knee in the kicking leg of a football player as he executes the kick.

[6 marks]

Joint type	
Articulating bones	
Plane of movement	
Movement	
Agonist	
Antagonist	

This question requires knowledge of the knee joint and an analysis of the execution phase of the kick. This is when the football player swings his leg forward to make contact with the ball. Make sure you look carefully at each of the headings before you complete the table.

Student A

Joint type	Hinge ✓
Articulating bones	Femur and tibia ✓
Plane of movement	Sagittal ✓
Movement	Extension ✓
Agonist	Rectus femoris ✓
Antagonist	Biceps femoris ✓

6/6 marks awarded Student A has correctly analysed the position of the knee as the ball is kicked using the headings in the table.

Student B

Joint type	Hinge ✓
Articulating bones	Femur, tibia and patella
Plane of movement	Sagittal ✓
Movement	Extension ✓
Agonist	Quadriceps
Antagonist	Hamstrings

3/6 marks awarded Student B has made a common mistake with the knee joint by including the patella. This is not an articulating bone at the knee joint. It meets at the joint but does not move. In addition, the answer refers to quadriceps and hamstrings. This is too vague — you must name one of the quadriceps and one of the hamstrings.

Question 2

Describe the nervous stimulation of a motor unit.

[3 marks]

To answer this question, you need to explain what a motor unit is and then describe how it works.

Student A

A motor unit is made up of a motor neurone and the muscle fibres it stimulates ✓. An action potential travels down the motor neurone ✓ to the neuromuscular junction ✓. Here the action potential crosses the synaptic cleft with the help of a neurotransmitter called acetylcholine ✓ and into the muscle fibre to create a contraction.

3/3 marks awarded This answer makes more than the required scoring points. Student A has explained in detail, using key words and terminology, how a motor unit is stimulated.

Student B

A motor unit consists of a motor neurone and muscle fibres ✓. It is stimulated when an impulse travels through the neurone to the muscle fibres, so they contract.

1/3 marks awarded Student B correctly identifies what a motor unit is, but is then too vague in their description of how a motor unit is stimulated. Key terminology needs to be used to score more marks.

Question 3

Identify the main muscle fibre type used by a 100 m sprinter, and give three functional characteristics of this fibre type.   [4 marks]

You need to name the correct fibre type and then give three functional (not structural) characteristics. A structural characteristic refers to the make-up of the fibre type and a functional characteristic is what it does. The question also only asks for three characteristics, so only your first three answers will be accepted.

Student A

A sprinter would mainly use fast glycolytic fibres ✓. This is because they produce the most force ✓ and have the fastest contraction speed ✓. However, they are also quick to fatigue ✓.

4/4 marks awarded Fast glycolytic fibres have been correctly identified and then only functional characteristics have been given.

Student B

A sprinter would use fast-twitch fibres in their race. These fibres have a large motor neurone size, low capillary density, high phosphocreatine store and a fast contraction speed.

0/4 marks awarded Fast-twitch fibres are identified but this is too general. The answer needs to be more specific and identify which type of fast-twitch fibre. Student B then identifies four characteristics of fast-twitch fibres but has not differentiated between structural and functional characteristics. The first three that are identified are all structural characteristics, so not creditworthy. The fourth answer correctly identifies a functional characteristic but the question asks for three characteristics, so the fourth answer is not counted. Always read a question carefully and highlight key words to help you in your answer. In this case, highlighting 'functional' might have enabled the student to correctly identify the creditworthy characteristics. In addition, highlighting 'three' would have ensured that three responses were given.

Cardiovascular and respiratory systems

Question 4

Describe the neural control of the heart during exercise.   [4 marks]

Neural control involves the autonomic nervous system. To answer this question you need to discuss the role of the receptors with regard to the cardiac control centre and the sympathetic system.

Student A

During exercise, baroreceptors detect a rise in blood pressure ✓, chemoreceptors detect an increase in acidity ✓ and proprioceptors detect an increase in muscle movement ✓. These all send impulses to the cardiac control centre, which controls heart rate ✓. This then sends impulses through the sympathetic nervous system via the accelerator nerve ✓, which stimulates the SA node ✓ to increase heart rate ✓.

4/4 marks awarded This is a comprehensive, detailed answer, which makes more than enough scoring points. Student A has correctly explained the role of the receptors, the cardiac control centre and the sympathetic system in working together to increase heart rate during exercise.

Student B

Baroreceptors, chemoreceptors and proprioceptors detect changes during exercise and send impulses to the brain. The brain then sends impulses down the sympathetic system ✓ and the SA node is stimulated, causing the heart to beat faster ✓.

2/4 marks awarded What is written is correct, but lacks the detail needed for full marks. Student B needs to describe what the three types of receptors detect — for example, proprioceptors detect an increase in muscle movement. Using the 'brain' is too vague; the part of the brain (cardiac control centre) must be specified.

Question 5

During a game of netball, the centre player works at various intensities. Describe how cardiac output increases when the netball performer is working at high intensity in the match.   [4 marks]

In this question remember the equation: cardiac output = heart rate × stroke volume. In order for cardiac output to increase, heart rate and stroke volume must increase, giving you 2 easy marks.

Student A

In the netball match the player's cardiac output increases when working at high intensity due to the increase in impulses from the sympathetic system ✓. This sends impulses to the SA node to increase its rate of firing ✓, so heart rate increases ✓. The heart will also have a stronger contraction ✓ and this will result in an increase in stroke volume ✓.

4/4 marks awarded This answer makes more than enough scoring points. Student A has correctly identified how cardiac output increases. Answers could also refer to increased levels of carbon dioxide, the release of adrenaline and an increased diastolic filling of the ventricles.

Student B

Cardiac output increases because the netball player needs more blood to go to her muscles, so that they receive more oxygen. This will mean that she can work at higher intensities throughout the whole game.

0/4 marks awarded Student B has made a common error and not read the question carefully, referring to why cardiac output increases, not how. Always highlight key words in the question so that you are clearer on what is required.

Question 6

Describe the mechanisms of breathing at rest and explain how these change during exercise.   [5 marks]

In this question you need to explain inspiration and expiration, both at rest and during exercise, and name the relevant respiratory muscles.

Student A

At rest, inspiration is active when the diaphragm and external intercostal muscles contract ✓, increasing the volume of the thoracic cavity and lowering the pressure so that air is moved into the lungs ✓. Breathing out at rest is passive ✓. During exercise, the mechanics of breathing change because more muscles are used. The extra inspiratory muscles are the sternocleidomastoid, scalenes and pectoralis minor ✓, and the effect of using more muscles increases the volume of the thoracic cavity to create a larger concentration gradient between inside the lungs and outside the body; therefore, air enters the lungs more quickly ✓. Expiration becomes active during exercise ✓ where the extra expiratory muscles are the internal intercostals and the rectus abdominus ✓.

5/5 marks awarded In this question there are 3 marks for describing breathing at rest and 2 marks for the changes during exercise. This is a top answer, which correctly identifies the extra muscles used during exercise and the effect this has on breathing. Student A has also identified when breathing is active or passive. They could have also mentioned that a decrease in volume of the thoracic cavity increases pressure in the lungs so that air is forced out quickly.

Student B

At rest, to get air into the lungs, the volume increases to lower the pressure ✓. This is done by the contraction of the intercostal muscles. When breathing out, these relax. This changes during exercise as more muscles are involved.

1/5 marks awarded This answer requires more detail. Just stating the intercostal muscles is not sufficient. The answer needs to specify which intercostal muscles (external for inspiration and internal for expiration). Expiration at rest is passive, which does mean the muscles relax, but to score a mark the correct terminology (passive) needs to be used. During exercise you must know which extra muscles are used and name them in your answer.

Question 7

In order to make use of their stamina, footballers need to take in oxygen. The diagram below shows values for the partial pressure of oxygen and carbon dioxide at two different locations in one gas exchange system.

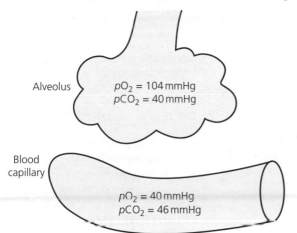

Alveolus

$pO_2 = 104$ mmHg
$pCO_2 = 40$ mmHg

Blood capillary

$pO_2 = 40$ mmHg
$pCO_2 = 46$ mmHg

Partial pressure in alveolus and blood vessel

Use the information from the diagram to explain how oxygen and carbon dioxide move between the two locations.

[3 marks]

You need to make sure that diffusion is defined and the movement of both gases is mentioned, using the values from the diagram. A typical mistake in gaseous exchange questions is to just include oxygen in the answer and omit carbon dioxide.

Student A

Both oxygen and carbon dioxide move between the alveoli and blood capillaries by diffusion, which is where a gas moves from an area of high concentration to an area of low concentration ✓. Oxygen moves from the alveolus where it is in high concentration (104 mm Hg) to the blood capillary where it is in low concentration (40 mm Hg) ✓. Carbon dioxide, on the other hand, moves in the opposite direction from the blood capillary where it is in high concentration (46 mm Hg) to the alveolus where it is in low concentration (40 mm Hg) ✓.

3/3 marks awarded Student A has correctly identified diffusion and defined it. They have then used the values in the diagram to explain how both oxygen and carbon dioxide move between the two locations.

Student B

Diffusion takes place. Oxygen moves from the alveolus to the blood capillary and carbon dioxide from the blood capillary to the alveolus ✓.

1/3 marks awarded Student B has not defined diffusion and has not used the values from the diagram to explain that both oxygen and carbon dioxide move from an area of high concentration to an area of low concentration.

Question 8

Explain the causes of the Bohr shift and identify the effect that this change has on oxygen delivery to the muscles. [4 marks]

In this question there are two parts to address — what causes the Bohr shift and how it affects oxygen delivery.

Student A

An increase in blood temperature ✓ and in the partial pressure of blood carbon dioxide ✓, as well as a low blood pH ✓ cause the Bohr shift. These all result in oxygen dissociating quickly and more readily from haemoglobin ✓.

4/4 marks awarded Student A has addressed both parts of the question, correctly identifying the causes of the Bohr shift and that this results in oxygen dissociating from haemoglobin more readily and thus increases oxygen uptake.

Student B

There are three factors that cause the Bohr shift: an increase in blood carbon dioxide ✓, an increase in blood temperature ✓ and a low blood pH caused by more carbon dioxide ✓.

3/4 marks awarded Student B has only addressed one part of the question. This is a common mistake in exams. If there is more than one part to a question, highlight them, as often when answering the first part you forget about the second or even third part and instead move on to the next question.

Energy for exercise

Question 9

An elite, world-class 400 m sprinter will complete the race in a time below 45 seconds. Explain how the majority of energy is provided during the race. [6 marks]

This question wants you to describe one of the three energy systems. Look at the intensity and duration of a sporting example when deciding which energy system to describe. The key word here is majority, because more than one energy system is used and you have to choose the main one.

Student A

The sprinter will use the glycolytic system ✓. This is an anaerobic reaction occurring in the sarcoplasm ✓ where PFK ✓ is the enzyme that is responsible for glycolysis ✓, in which glycogen is first converted into glucose, which is broken down to pyruvic acid ✓. The pyruvic acid is then converted to the by-product lactic acid ✓ and the one mole of glycogen produces 2 ATP ✓.

6/6 marks awarded This answer correctly identifies the glycolytic system as the main system for producing energy during the race, and then describes the key points you need to know for this system.

Student B

The 400 m sprinter will use the ATP-PC system. This is anaerobic and occurs in the sarcoplasm where creatine kinase is the enzyme that breaks down the PC that is stored in the muscles into creatine and phosphate. One ATP is produced.

0/6 marks awarded Student B has identified an incorrect energy system. The ATP-PC system is used during the 400 m but it is not the dominant system. Always look at intensity and duration when deciding on the main energy system for energy production. In this case the 400 m needs energy for high-intensity activity, as the question mentions sprinting and the duration is approximately 45 seconds. The ATP-PC system can only provide energy for up to 10 seconds, which means that it cannot be the main system used during the race.

Question 10

Define what is meant by the term 'energy continuum' and explain where on the energy continuum you would place the following activities:

- 100 m
- 400 m
- 3000 m

[5 marks]

There are 2 marks available for defining the term 'energy continuum'. You then need to identify and explain the main energy system used for the 100 m, 400 m and 3000 m. To do this, think of the intensity and duration of these athletic events.

Student A

The energy continuum explains the contribution of each energy system ✓ to overall energy production, depending on the intensity and duration of the activity ✓. The 100 m uses the ATP-PC system because it is a high-intensity event and has a short duration of around 10 seconds ✓. The 400 m uses the glycolytic system because the intensity is high and the duration longer, at around 50 seconds ✓. The 3000 m uses the aerobic system because this event is more enduring and is run at a lower intensity ✓.

5/5 marks awarded This answer correctly defines the energy continuum and refers to intensity and duration when justifying which event uses which energy system.

Student B

The energy continuum is the contribution of each energy system ✓ depending on the duration and intensity of exercise ✓. The 100 m uses the ATP-PC system to provide energy, the 400 m uses the glycolytic system and the 3000 m uses the aerobic system.

2/5 marks awarded This answer correctly defines the energy continuum and also identifies correctly which energy system is the main energy provider for each of the athletic events. However, it fails to score marks for this as it only identifies, and the question asks for an explanation. To score the marks, Student B needed to explain the intensity and duration of each athletic event in relation to the energy system used.

Environmental effects on body systems

Question 11

Evaluate whether high-altitude training is beneficial for an endurance athlete. [8 marks]

> This question asks you to evaluate, so you need to say what altitude training is and give both the advantages and disadvantages of altitude training and its impact on an endurance athlete.

Student A

At high altitude, above 2500 m, the partial pressure of oxygen is lower ✓. This results in haemoglobin not being fully saturated, which lowers the oxygen carrying capacity of the blood ✓. At first the endurance athlete could suffer from altitude sickness ✓, poor sleep and headaches ✓. Detraining will also occur at first because the decreased amount of oxygen will mean the endurance athlete will not be able to train at the same intensity ✓.

Therefore, in order to gain any benefits from high-altitude training, the endurance athlete will have to acclimatise ✓. As a result they will have an increase in red blood cells and EPO ✓. They will also have a greater concentration of haemoglobin ✓ and an increase in capillarisation ✓. All of these will increase the oxygen carrying capacity of the blood ✓ and mean that the endurance athlete can work at a higher intensity, aerobically, for longer ✓.

8/8 marks awarded This answer provides more than enough scoring points. It correctly identifies what altitude training is and then evaluates whether it is beneficial for an endurance athlete by giving the advantages, but also stressing the importance of acclimatisation, otherwise there are disadvantages that could impact on an endurance athlete.

Student B

Altitude training is beneficial for an endurance athlete because it helps to improve their aerobic capacity or stamina ✓. This is because training at altitude increases the number of red blood cells ✓, results in a higher concentration of haemoglobin ✓, and increases capillary density around the muscles and lungs ✓.

4/8 marks awarded Marks are lost here because the answer only gives the benefits of altitude training. The question asks you to *evaluate*, so this means give both sides, which in this case means advantages and disadvantages.

Question 12

During a marathon in hot conditions, temperature regulation can be a problem. Why does an increase in body temperature cause problems and how could a marathon runner regulate their temperature during a race? [6 marks]

> This requires you to explain how an increase in temperature can have an effect on the cardiovascular and respiratory systems of the marathon runner, and then give a description of how temperature is regulated.

Student A

Muscle contractions cause heat during a marathon, which raises core body temperature ✓. If the runner does not control this, they can enter hyperthermia ✓, which leads to a decrease in venous return and in stroke volume ✓. Sweating becomes less efficient, so dehydration occurs ✓. In the respiratory system the airways become dry, which makes breathing more difficult. To regulate temperature during the race, thermoreceptors detect the increases in temperature in hot conditions ✓ and send impulses to the thermoregulatory centre ✓. This causes the blood vessels near the surface of the skin to vasodilate ✓ and heat evaporates through sweating ✓.

6/6 marks awarded There is a sub-max for this question, with 3 marks available for how an increase in body temperature can cause problems and 3 marks for temperature regulation. This answer scores more than the marks available for each sub-max, correctly identifying the effect of a high body temperature on the cardiovascular and respiratory systems. Although the question does not ask for the effect on the cardiovascular and respiratory systems, the specification requires this knowledge.

Student B

During a marathon, core body temperature increases and this results in hyperthermia ✓, where venous return and stroke volume decrease ✓ and so do blood pressure and cardiac output ✓. In the respiratory system, breathing increases because there is less oxygen being transported to the muscles ✓.

3/6 marks awarded Student B has answered the first part well, scoring full marks for the sub-max, but they have made the common mistake of not addressing both parts of the question. Always read the question carefully and check your response to make sure all parts of the question have been answered.

Exercise physiology

Diet and nutrition and their effect on physical activity and sport

Question 13

Explain how the diet of a power athlete may differ from that of an endurance athlete. [4 marks]

> Look at the energy demands of the power athlete and an endurance athlete when answering this question, as this will help you to decide which food groups are most important.

Student A

A power athlete will need to eat more protein ✓ for muscle growth and repair ✓ due to the high intensity of their activity. An endurance athlete will participate for longer, so will need more energy-based ✓ foods such as carbohydrates and good fats ✓.

4/4 marks awarded The difference in diet is identified and an explanation given as to why these foods are more important for the power and endurance athletes.

Student B

A power athlete will eat more protein ✓ and an endurance athlete will eat more carbohydrates ✓.

2/4 marks awarded This answer has lost 2 easy marks because Student B has identified the difference in diet but not explained the reasons why.

Question 14

Evaluate the use of caffeine supplements to maximise performance. [4 marks]

> This question asks you to evaluate, which means you need to look at both the advantages and disadvantages of taking caffeine, and apply the advantages to maximising performance.

Student A

Caffeine can increase mental alertness ✓ and can also reduce fatigue ✓. Caffeine can also improve the mobilisation of fatty acids ✓ and therefore spare glycogen stores ✓. This means it is suitable for use by endurance performers who predominantly use fats, which are the preferred energy source for aerobic exercise over a long duration ✓. However, caffeine can also cause dehydration ✓, insomnia ✓ and diarrhoea ✓.

4/4 marks awarded This answer provides more than enough scoring points. Student A has evaluated by giving both the positives and negatives of caffeine, and also related the use of caffeine to an endurance performer.

Student B

Caffeine can help maximise endurance performance because it mobilises fatty acids ✓, spares glycogen stores ✓, reduces fatigue and increases mental alertness.

2/4 marks awarded Although this answer gives four correct answers on the positives of using caffeine, the question asks for evaluation of the use of caffeine, so there is a sub-max of 2 marks for the advantages and a sub-max of 2 marks for the disadvantages. Always look carefully at the command term in the question, in this case *evaluate*, as it will help you to structure your answer correctly and ensure that you cover everything.

Question 15

Some elite performers are tempted to break the rules and use steroids to enhance their performance. Describe the reasons why an elite performer may choose to use a pharmacological aid such as steroids to enhance their performance. [3 marks]

This question is simply asking how steroids can enhance performance, so although it is illegal, you need to give the benefits of using steroids.

3/3 marks awarded Three possible benefits of taking steroids are correctly stated.

Student A

Steroids are more likely to be used by power athletes because they can increase strength ✓. They also allow a performer to train harder for longer ✓ and speed up recovery ✓.

Student B

Steroids increase muscle mass ✓, strength and enhance recovery ✓.

2/3 marks awarded Student B thinks they have given three different answers, but an increase in strength and muscle mass is the same point on the mark scheme. In your revision it is worth checking past mark schemes so you avoid this type of mistake.

Preparation and training methods

Question 16

A marathon is run over 42.2 km, so a high VO_2 max is therefore important for success. Define the term VO_2 max and explain three physiological factors that allow for a high VO_2 max. [4 marks]

To answer this question you need to provide an accurate definition of VO_2 max, identify changes in the body for a marathon runner and then explain how these help them to have a high VO_2 max. Only give three factors because only the first three will be creditworthy.

Student A

VO_2 max is the maximum volume of oxygen that can be taken up and used by the muscles per minute ✓. A marathon runner will have a high VO_2 max because they have more haemoglobin and red blood cells, so can transport more oxygen ✓. They will have more myoglobin, so will be able to store more oxygen in the muscles ✓ and will have an increase in lactate tolerance, so will be able to work at a higher intensity for longer ✓.

4/4 marks awarded Student A has correctly defined VO_2 max, given three physiological factors and explained how these lead to a high VO_2 max.

Student B

VO_2 max is the maximum amount of air that can be taken in during 1 minute. Three factors that affect VO_2 max are training, gender and age.

0/4 marks awarded The definition is incorrect. VO_2 max is not about taking air in but how it is used by the muscles. The factors that have been given are correct, but the question asks for *physiological* factors; these are general factors. Try to highlight key words so you can ensure that the correct content is addressed in your answers.

Question 17

Identify which type of strength is most important for a weightlifter and explain the factors that enable the weightlifter to maximise their strength in competition. [3 marks]

> You need to decide which of the four types of strength on the specification is the most important for the weightlifter and then explain the factors that affect their strength.

Student A

Maximum strength is the most important for the weightlifter ✓. In order to lift heavy weights the weightlifter will use fast-twitch fibres because these can produce more power and maximum strength ✓. Their muscles will also have a greater cross-sectional area, which means they can produce more strength ✓.

3/3 marks awarded This answer correctly identifies the type of strength that is most important for a weightlifter and then applies the factors affecting their strength that allow them to maximise their performance in competition.

Student B

Explosive strength is important for a weightlifter. The factors that affect their strength are fibre type and cross-sectional area.

0/3 marks awarded The definition of explosive strength is the ability to overcome resistance with a high speed of contraction, which is more suitable for the long jump. Student B has correctly given the two factors that affect strength, but has not scored any marks because they have not explained what fibre type or what cross-sectional area is needed to enable the weightlifter to maximise their performance.

Question 18

Identify three factors that affect flexibility. [3 marks]

> This is a simple recall question, which asks for three factors. The examiner will only mark your first three answers.

Student A

Three factors that affect flexibility are the type of joint ✓, age ✓ and gender ✓.

3/3 marks awarded Three correct factors are identified. The other factor is the elasticity of the surrounding tissue.

Student B

Age ✓ and gender ✓ can affect flexibility.

2/3 marks awarded A simple recall question depends on the detail in your revision. Student B either did not revise thoroughly enough or did not check their answer to make sure they had stated three factors and not just two.

Question 19

Explain how periodisation can be used to structure a performer's competitive year. [6 marks]

> This question is asking you to identify and explain the three cycles of periodisation and the three phases of training. You need to give details of what to include in each.

Student A

Periodisation is dividing the training year into sections in which specific training takes place ✓. There is the macrocycle, which is the long-term performance goal ✓. This includes the preparation period, which is just before the competitive season takes place and concentrates on fitness. ✓ In the competition period, which is the season itself, skills are the main focus ✓. Then there is the transition period, which is at the end of the season and when the performer rests ✓. The mesocycle is a period of between 4 and 12 weeks where the emphasis is on something specific such as strength ✓ and a microcycle is a description of one week of training ✓.

6/6 marks awarded This answer provides more than enough scoring points. Student A correctly identifies the three cycles of periodisation as the macrocycle, mesocycle and microcycle, and the three phases of training as the preparation period, competitive period and transition period. They also explain what is involved in each of these.

Student B

Periodisation includes the macrocycle, mesocycle and microcycle ✓. The three phases of training are the preparatory period, the competitive period and the transition period ✓.

2/6 marks awarded Student B has correctly identified the three cycles of periodisation and the three phases of training but has not gone on to explain what these mean.

Question 20

Evaluate the impact of continuous training on lifestyle diseases of the respiratory system.   [2 marks]

Be careful when answering this question — it is asking for the impact of training on lifestyle diseases of the *respiratory* system.

Student A

Continuous training decreases the risk of COPD because it maintains full use of lung tissue and elasticity ✓. It also strengthens the respiratory muscles, which helps asthma sufferers ✓.

2/2 marks awarded The effects of continuous training on lifestyle diseases of the respiratory system are correctly identified.

Student B

Continuous training can help people with asthma because the respiratory muscles are strengthened ✓, and it can also reduce the risk of coronary heart disease.

1/2 marks awarded Student B has made a common error and named only one respiratory disease in their answer. Although continuous training reduces the risks of coronary heart disease, this is not a respiratory disease.

Injury prevention and the rehabilitation of injury

Question 21

A warm-up is important in helping to minimise the risk of injury during competition. What other precautions can be taken to avoid injury?   [3 marks]

This question is worth 3 marks, so try to make sure you give at least three precautions. In the specification this comes under intrinsic and extrinsic risk factors.

Student A

First of all, to avoid injury it is important that the correct clothing and equipment are worn, for example shin pads in football ✓. It is also important to make sure training is progressive and does not overload the body too quickly ✓. Finally, correct technique is important so that there is not too much stress on the muscles ✓.

3/3 marks awarded This answer has correctly listed three other precautions that can be taken to avoid injury. Other answers might include good flexibility and correct nutrition.

Student B

It is important to make sure the correct clothing is worn, such as trainers ✓. Another precaution would be to wear protective clothing, such as a gum shield or a scrum cap in rugby. A third precaution is to ensure good flexibility, as this can help to avoid injury ✓.

2/3 marks awarded Although all three answers are correct, the first and second answer refer to clothing, which is one point on the mark scheme. Always check for similarity in your answers. If you are not sure, and the question does not specify a certain number, then give an extra answer.

Question 22

A fracture is an acute injury that needs immediate attention. Identify the correct medical treatment that a sports coach should apply to a fracture injury. [3 marks]

This question is asking for the medical treatment a sports coach should give, so only include the steps a coach would take to treat a fracture.

Student A

The first thing the coach needs to do is get medical help and call for an ambulance ✓. They need to support the injured area if it helps the patient, and keep them still ✓. If they have any pain medication, this can also be given to the injured person ✓.

3/3 marks awarded Three correct treatment methods are given.

Student B

A fracture will need medical attention ✓. The injured person will be in a lot of pain, so the injury needs to be kept still ✓. When in hospital the fracture will be immobilised and put into a plaster cast and if they cannot put weight on it they will also be given crutches. Sometimes surgery is needed to repair a fracture, depending on how bad a fracture it is.

2/3 marks awarded Student B has given two correct answers when identifying the medical treatment the coach can administer, but then goes on to describe hospital treatment for a fracture. This information is correct, but is not what the question is asking for. It is often helpful to highlight key words in a question. Had this student highlighted the word *coach* they may well have avoided describing hospital treatment.

Question 23

In a game of rugby, two 17-year-old players have a serious head clash in a tackle. The coach has recognised that his players may be concussed. What medical treatment should these two players receive? [4 marks]

To answer this question you need to consider which parts of the 'recognise and remove' campaign (six Rs) are creditworthy, and explain them.

Student A

The first thing the coach should do is remove the players from the field ✓. These players then need to be referred to a qualified person who is trained in concussion ✓. For the first 24 hours the players need to rest and must not be left alone ✓. As they are 17 they must be left to recover for a minimum of 2 weeks ✓. They can only return to play when they are symptom-free and have completed the graduated return to play protocol ✓.

4/4 marks awarded Student A correctly identifies the five Rs that are relevant (the first one — 'recognise' — has already been mentioned in the wording of the question.

Student B

When there is a concussion injury it is important to follow the six Rs. The first thing is to recognise the signs of concussion, and then remove the player from the pitch ✓. The player then needs to be rested for 24 hours and not left on their own ✓. Finally, they need to be left to recover and if they are symptom-free for 1 week they then need to see a doctor to see if they can return to playing.

2/4 marks awarded The first R in Student B's answer is correct, but the question states that the concussion injury has been recognised, so this part is not creditworthy. The second error is not taking into account the age of the rugby players. At 17 they have to recover for 2 weeks, not 1 week, so this answer has not been applied correctly.

■ Biomechanics

Biomechanical principles, levers and the use of technology

Question 24

Explain Newton's first and second laws of motion in relation to the shot put.　　　[6 marks]

> When answering this question make sure you explain just the first and second laws of motion. You need to know which law is which.

Student A

Newton's first law of inertia states that 'every body continues in its state of rest or motion in a straight line, unless compelled to change that state by external forces exerted upon it' ✓. In terms of the shot, it will remain in the thrower's hand in a state of rest until the shot putter exerts a muscular force on it ✓. Also, the shot will continue to act as a projectile in a state of motion until it hits the ground ✓.

Newton's second law of acceleration states that 'the rate of momentum of a body (or the acceleration for a body of constant mass) is proportional to the force causing it and the change that takes place in the direction in which the force acts' ✓. Force = mass × acceleration ($F = ma$). ✓ When the shot putter exerts a muscular force to throw the shot, the acceleration of the shot or its rate of change of momentum is proportional to the size of the force ✓. So, the greater the muscular force from the throwing arm, the faster and further the shot will go ✓.

6/6 marks awarded This answer provides more than enough scoring points. Student A has correctly selected Newton's first law of inertia and second law of acceleration. They have then gone on to show thorough knowledge of these two laws and the ability to apply those laws to the shot put.

Student B

Newton's first law of inertia states that 'every body continues in its state of rest or motion in a straight line, unless compelled to change that state by external forces exerted upon it' ✓. So, for example, the shot will remain in the thrower's hand until the shot putter extends their arm and exerts a muscular force on the shot ✓. Newton's second law is the law of reaction, where for every action force there is an equal and opposite reaction force. In terms of the shot, the action force comes from the hand.

2/6 marks awarded Student B has discussed Newton's third law of motion (law of action/reaction) instead of the second law. Make sure you are aware of which law is which, as this is a common mistake. They have also described the first law correctly and applied their knowledge to the shot, but have only scored 2 marks. Look at how many marks a question is worth. Had they checked the mark allocation they might have gained another mark for more application.

Question 25

Identify and explain two forces acting on a triple jumper at take-off.　　　[4 marks]

> In this question you need to identify the forces as weight or gravity, air resistance or friction, and explain the effect that each of these has on the triple jumper.

Student A

One force acting on a triple jumper is weight ✓, which acts in a downward direction, pushing the performer back towards the track and the sand pit ✓. Another force is air resistance ✓, which acts in a horizontal direction, opposing motion ✓.

4/4 marks awarded Student A has correctly identified two forces and then goes on to explain the effect they have on the triple jumper. They could also have chosen friction, which occurs when the triple jumper's spikes make contact with the track, allowing them to move forward.

Student B

The two forces acting on the triple jumper are weight ✓ and friction ✓.

2/4 marks awarded Student B has only addressed one part of the question. This is a common mistake in exams and in this case loses 2 marks. They have only identified the forces and not explained them. Always read the question carefully and highlight the command terms to ensure that your answer covers all aspects of the question.

Question 26

Good stability is important in team games. Using a game of your choice, explain the factors that need to be considered to increase stability.

[3 marks]

Here you need to identify the factors that affect stability that are on the specification, and then explain how they are used by a games player.

Student A

As a rugby player prepares for a tackle, they need to make sure they lower their centre of mass to make them more stable on contact ✓. They also need to give their support a base wide ✓. Their line of gravity needs to be centred over their feet ✓. Also, the more weight the rugby player has, the more stable they will become ✓.

3/3 marks awarded This answer provides more than enough scoring points. The factors that affect stability are correctly identified and explained in relation to the rugby player preparing to tackle.

Student B

A gymnast needs to be stable on landing, so first of all they will need to lower their centre of mass on contact with the ground. Then they will make sure that their base of support is wide, to increase stability with two points of contact (both feet). In addition, their line of gravity needs to be directly over their base of support to also make their landing more stable.

0/3 marked awarded This answer correctly identifies three factors that affect stability, but scores no marks because the practical example they have used is a gymnast and not a games player. Always look at the practical example in the question, and make sure you use this in your answer.

Question 27

Name and sketch the lever system that operates during plantarflexion of the ankle.

[3 marks]

You need to decide which class of lever system plantarflexion of the ankle belongs to — first, second or third. After naming the lever system you need to sketch it, putting the fulcrum, resistance and effort in the correct order.

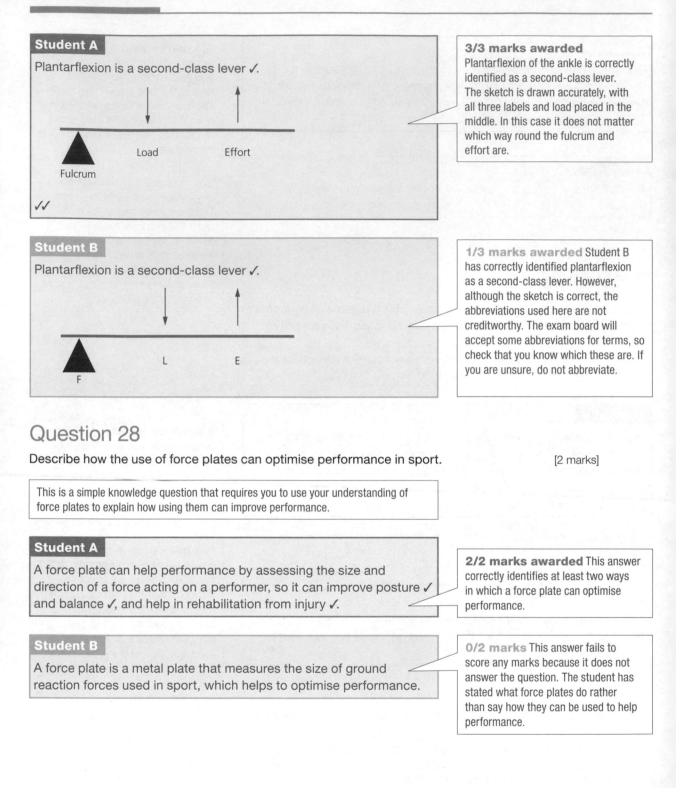

Student A

Plantarflexion is a second-class lever ✓.

Load   Effort

Fulcrum

✓✓

3/3 marks awarded
Plantarflexion of the ankle is correctly identified as a second-class lever. The sketch is drawn accurately, with all three labels and load placed in the middle. In this case it does not matter which way round the fulcrum and effort are.

Student B

Plantarflexion is a second-class lever ✓.

L   E

F

1/3 marks awarded Student B has correctly identified plantarflexion as a second-class lever. However, although the sketch is correct, the abbreviations used here are not creditworthy. The exam board will accept some abbreviations for terms, so check that you know which these are. If you are unsure, do not abbreviate.

Question 28

Describe how the use of force plates can optimise performance in sport.   [2 marks]

This is a simple knowledge question that requires you to use your understanding of force plates to explain how using them can improve performance.

Student A

A force plate can help performance by assessing the size and direction of a force acting on a performer, so it can improve posture ✓ and balance ✓, and help in rehabilitation from injury ✓.

2/2 marks awarded This answer correctly identifies at least two ways in which a force plate can optimise performance.

Student B

A force plate is a metal plate that measures the size of ground reaction forces used in sport, which helps to optimise performance.

0/2 marks This answer fails to score any marks because it does not answer the question. The student has stated what force plates do rather than say how they can be used to help performance.

Linear motion, angular motion, fluid mechanics and projectile motion

Question 29

The effect of a force when applied by a performer can determine the type of motion produced. Using an example from a team game of your choice, explain how a performer could produce:

(a) linear motion

(b) angular motion

[4 marks]

To answer this question you need to explain how different types of motion can be produced, depending on where the force is applied in relation to the centre of mass. Make sure you apply your knowledge to a team game.

Student A

(a) Linear motion is when a force is applied through the centre of mass ✓, for example a force straight through the centre of a ball will make it move in a straight line in the direction in which the force was applied ✓.

(b) Angular motion is when a force is applied off-centre and outside the centre of mass ✓, for example in a free kick, kicking the ball at the side will create a spin or curve, which is used to try to confuse the goalkeeper ✓.

4/4 marks awarded A correct explanation on how to produce each type of motion is given and there is a relevant example to accompany both linear motion and angular motion.

Student B

(a) Linear motion is movement in a straight line.

(b) Angular movement is rotational movement. In tennis you can create top-spin and back-spin by hitting the ball at the side, outside the centre of mass ✓.

1/4 marks awarded Student B has explained *what* linear and angular motion are instead of saying *how* they are produced. There is only one example given, so another mark is lost. If the question asks for examples, make sure you give all of them.

Question 30

In mechanical terms, angular momentum = moment of inertia × angular velocity. Use your understanding of this equation to explain how a spinning trampoline performer is able to perform a greater number of tucked somersaults than straight somersaults during flight.

[6 marks]

You need to explain each of the key terms in the equation. Then you need to apply them in relation to the spinning trampoline performer when performing a tucked somersault and a straight somersault.

Student A

Angular momentum is a conserved quantity of rotation ✓. Moment of inertia is the resistance of a body to change its state of angular motion or rotation ✓, and angular velocity refers to the speed of the spin ✓. In a straight-body position the trampoline performer distributes their mass away from the transverse axis, so their moment of inertia is high and angular velocity is low ✓. In the tucked position their mass moves closer to the transverse axis, so moment of inertia is low and angular velocity is high ✓. This means that the trampoline performer is able to do more tucked somersaults in flight than straight somersaults, because they are faster ✓.

6/6 marks awarded This answer correctly explains angular momentum, moment of inertia and angular velocity and then applies these terms to a tucked and straight somersault in order to identify how a tucked somersault is quicker, thus allowing the trampoline performer to complete more in flight.

Student B

A trampoline performer brings their arms and legs in to perform a tucked somersault and this allows them to go faster ✓. This means they can perform more tucked somersaults than straight somersaults in flight ✓.

2/6 marks awarded Student B has lost marks by omitting key terminology. The answer does not make it clear that it is referring to moment of inertia and angular velocity. The question asks students to use the equation, but this answer fails to do so. Always read a question carefully. If it asks you to refer to something, check your answer to make sure you have.

Question 31

Explain the Bernoulli principle in relation to an upward lift force for a discus thrower. [4 marks]

To answer this question you need to explain airflow above and below the discus, and identify how this creates an upward lift force on the discus.

Student A

An upward lift force during flight means the discus can stay in the air for longer, which increases the horizontal distance it travels ✓. In terms of the Bernoulli principle, the air that travels over the top of the discus has to travel a longer distance than the air underneath ✓. This means the air above the discus travels faster, which therefore creates a lower pressure ✓. The air that travels under the discus has to travel a shorter distance than the air above. This means the air below the discus travels more slowly, which therefore creates a higher pressure ✓. The higher pressure below the discus then creates an upward lift force and allows the discus to travel further. When the discus is released, the angle of attack is important ✓. The optimum angle of attack is anything between 25 and 40 degrees ✓.

4/4 marks awarded This answer provides more than enough scoring points. Bernoulli's principle is described correctly and applied to the discus throw. In addition, Student A explains the importance of the angle of attack and gives an example.

Student B

The discus has an upward lift force, because the air that travels over the top of the discus travels a shorter distance than the air underneath. As a result, the air above the discus travels at a slower velocity and a higher pressure. This creates an upward lift force.

0/4 marks awarded This answer scores no marks because the student has described how a downward lift force is created. This is a simple mistake to make. High pressure causes lift, so the high pressure needs to be underneath the discus if it is to produce an upward lift force.

Question 32

In a game of badminton, a performer will hit the shuttlecock into the air to cross the net, and it then becomes a projectile. Explain how the various forces act to affect the shuttlecock during its flight.

[3 marks]

In this question you need to identify the forces as weight or gravity and air resistance, and explain the effect that each of these has on the flight path of the shuttlecock. When weight is the larger of the two forces the projectile follows a parabolic flight path, and if air resistance is the larger of the two forces a non-parabolic flight path is the result.

Student A

Two external forces act on the shuttlecock. Weight or gravity reduces height because it pushes the shuttlecock downwards, acting on the vertical component ✓. Air resistance opposes motion ✓ and acts on the horizontal component. This will have a big effect on the shuttlecock because it is light and has an irregular shape ✓. When air resistance is the bigger of the two forces, which is the case with a shuttlecock, it will follow a non-parabolic flight path ✓.

3/3 marks awarded This answer provides more than enough scoring points. Student A has correctly identified weight/gravity and air resistance as the two forces that act on a projectile. They have then applied this knowledge by explaining the effect these two forces have on the shuttlecock and the flight path the shuttlecock consequently takes.

Student B

Gravity pushes the shuttlecock towards the ground ✓ and air resistance opposes motion ✓.

2/3 marks awarded The forces are correctly identified but more application to the shuttlecock and its flight path is needed for full marks.

■ Extended synoptic 20-mark questions

Question 33

An elite football player requires a large aerobic capacity to perform effectively throughout the duration of a match. They also need to be able to recover quickly.

Explain why a high aerobic capacity is important and describe how excess post-exercise oxygen consumption (EPOC) helps the player to recover and maintain performance.

Explain and evaluate how glycogen-loading will prepare the football player to perform effectively throughout the match.

[20 marks]

> This is an extended synoptic question that requires you to draw together knowledge from more than one topic within component 01. EPOC is covered in the energy and exercise topic, aerobic capacity can be found in preparation and training methods, and glycogen loading is in diet and nutrition. There are 7 **AO1** marks available, 7 **AO2** marks and 6 **AO3** marks.

Student A

Aerobic capacity is the ability of the body to inspire, transport and utilise oxygen to perform sustained periods of aerobic activity **AO1**. A game of football is predominantly an aerobic activity because the game lasts 90 minutes **AO2**. A high aerobic capacity means that more oxygen is available **AO1**, which will prevent the build-up of lactic acid **AO1** and therefore delay OBLA **AO3**. As a result, the football player will be able to play at a higher intensity for longer **AO2**. A high aerobic capacity also means they will have an increased oxygen carrying capacity to their muscles due to having more red blood cells **AO1**.

The football player will also be able to recover quicker as more oxygen will be supplied to the muscles during EPOC **AO1**. EPOC is the volume of oxygen consumed in recovery above what would normally be consumed at rest **AO1**. There are two components in EPOC. The first is the fast component, also called the alactacid component **AO1**. This component involves the resaturation of myoglobin with oxygen **AO1** and the resynthesis of ATP and phosphocreatine levels **AO1**. This component uses approximately 2–4 litres of oxygen **AO1** and is completed in 3 minutes **AO1**. 50% of PC stores are replenished within 30 seconds **AO1**. During a game of football this allows the player to complete high-intensity exercise again within a short period of time, such as a sprint for the ball **AO2**. The second component is the slow component, also called the lactacid component. **AO1** This involves the removal of lactic acid **AO1**. Most of the lactic acid can be oxidised into carbon dioxide and water **AO1**. Some lactic acid can be converted to muscle glycogen, glucose and protein **AO1**. If the football player can maintain a higher heart rate and respiratory rate during EPOC **AO1** they will be able to remove some lactic acid during the game, which

17/20 marks awarded
Demonstrating more AO2 and AO3 knowledge in this level-4 response would have enabled full marks. To do this there needed to be more application, with well-argued judgements supported by practical examples, and there could have been more evaluation of glycogen-loading by looking at the negatives of using this method of supplementation. Other indicative content could include a discussion on VO_2 max, because this is a key component of aerobic capacity.

will stop them fatiguing as quickly AO2. Part of this component can therefore take place during the match when the intensity drops AO2, but most of this component takes place after the match. It can take up to 2 hours AO1 but allows the football player to reduce the impact of DOMS AO3.

Glycogen-loading can be used by the football player so that they can store more glycogen AO1. This means they will have a larger fuel store for aerobic energy production AO3, which means they will be able to increase their endurance AO3 and therefore will be able to delay fatigue AO3 and play at a higher intensity for the full 90 minutes AO2.

Student B

Aerobic capacity is the same as stamina and this is important for a football player to last for the full 90 minutes AO2. If the player has a good aerobic capacity, they will be able to transport more oxygen to their working muscles AO1, which means they will be able to work aerobically for longer and at a higher intensity, and not use anaerobic respiration as much, with its fatiguing by-products AO2.

EPOC is when you take in extra oxygen during recovery to restore the body and remove waste products to get the body back to normal. The waste products that are removed are lactic acid AO1.

Glycogen-loading can help the football player as it will delay fatigue AO3 and it will also improve their aerobic capacity as they will be able to work aerobically for longer AO3.

5/20 marks awarded Much of this level-1 answer is too vague. More detail is needed, for example referring to lactic acid rather than fatiguing by-products, and relating it to aerobic capacity, for example delaying OBLA and therefore allowing the football player to work more effectively at a higher intensity for longer aerobically. Simple marks have been lost by not defining key words or terms. If you see key terminology in a question, always show the examiner that you know what it means by defining it. There are also no attempts in this response to link EPOC and aerobic capacity. In addition, information on glycogen-loading is brief, with no evaluation, because only the benefits have been discussed.

Question 34

An elite 200 m sprinter runs 8 × 200 m sprints with 30-second recovery periods in an interval training session. Each sprint was completed in the following times:

Sprint 1	Sprint 2	Sprint 3	Sprint 4	Sprint 5	Sprint 6
23.1 s	23.3 s	23.6 s	24 s	24.5 s	25.1 s

How would the majority of the athlete's energy be supplied during each sprint? Explain why the time for the last sprint is slower than the first sprint.

Evaluate how creatine supplementation would help the sprinter.   [20 marks]

This extended synoptic question requires you to draw together knowledge from two topic areas within energy for exercise in component 01 and also knowledge from the diet and nutrition topic. To answer this question you need to decide on and then describe the main energy system or systems providing energy during the sprints and look at the recovery time to explain why the last sprint is slower. Then evaluate the use of creatine and how it will help in the 200 m sprint.

Student A

During the 200 m sprints the energy will be provided by the ATP-PC system AO2 and the glycolytic system AO2. This is because the 200 m is a high-intensity event with a short duration AO2, so energy needs to be provided quickly and the ATP-PC system is the quickest at producing energy, because it is a simple process AO3. Both of these systems are anaerobic AO1. In the ATP-PC system, creatine kinase is the controlling enzyme AO1 that breaks down phosphocreatine into phosphate and creatine AO1 in the sarcoplasm of the muscle AO1, with an energy yield of 1 ATP AO1. The glycolytic system will be used more in the second part of the 200 m as the ATP-PC system runs out AO2. This also occurs in the sarcoplasm of the muscle AO1, where PFK AO1 is the enzyme that is responsible for glycolysis AO1, when glycogen is first converted into glucose, which is then broken down to pyruvic acid AO1. The pyruvic acid is then converted to the by-product lactic acid AO1 and the 1 mole of glycogen produces 2 ATP AO1.

During the fast component of EPOC AO1 the recovery time for the sprints is not long enough to fully return the body back to its pre-exercise state AO2. A recovery of 30 seconds means that only 50% of phosphocreatine can be resynthesized AO3. The 30-second recovery is not long enough for full resynthesis, so this means that the ATP-PC system is used less and less and the glycolytic system more and more AO3. This is why the sprinter's times start to increase, because the glycolytic system produces a fatiguing by-product AO2 called lactic acid AO1. The sprinter will start to experience OBLA AO3 and this will cause them to slow down AO2. This is because the high blood acidity will cause enzymes to become denatured AO1, and this means that energy cannot be produced as efficiently towards the last few sprints, causing the athlete to tire, which is why the time increases AO2.

Taking creatine would increase the working duration of the ATP-PC system AO3, and this would mean that more energy could be provided with this system and therefore delay the use of the glycolytic system AO3. Consequently, this would delay fatigue as less lactic acid would be produced AO3. However, too much creatine can lead to water retention and muscle cramps AO3.

Student B

The 200 m uses the ATP-PC system for the first 10 seconds as this is the length of time that this system can provide energy for AO2. After this the sprinter then uses the glycolytic system for the rest of the sprint AO2. The ATP-PC system is an anaerobic system AO1, where phosphocreatine in the muscle is broken down to make 1 ATP AO1. The glycolytic system is also anaerobic AO1 and glycolysis takes place AO1, with 2 ATP produced AO1. The sprinter starts to slow down

20/20 marks awarded In this level-4 response Student A correctly identifies that both the ATP-PC system and glycolytic system are used during the sprints, and demonstrates detailed knowledge of the key points that are needed for each energy system. They have also applied their knowledge by stating that the major disadvantage of using the glycolytic energy system is the fatiguing effect of the by-product lactic acid, causing the athlete to reach OBLA due to insufficient recovery time. They have linked the length of the recovery time to the resynthesis of phosphocreatine, and have evaluated effectively the use of creatine to extend the use of the ATP-PC system in order to try to delay fatigue.

7/20 marks awarded This is a level-2 response. More marks would have been scored for giving greater detail for each of the energy systems. More detailed knowledge of each of the energy systems requires more in-depth revision. The harder part of this question is why the sprinter fatigues, which requires more application of knowledge, which this answer fails to do. There is no mention of the 30-second recovery time and the effect this has on the restoration of phosphocreatine. The use of creatine as a supplement is discussed only briefly. Greater evaluation would have involved identifying the benefits and risks associated with its use.

because they are fatiguing as they do more and more sprints. You can see this from the times, with the first sprint taking 23.1 seconds and the last sprint taking 25.1 seconds, which means the athlete has slowed down by two seconds.

Creatine can help the sprinter because it helps them use the ATP-PC system for longer AO3, which is the system they would prefer to use.

Question 35

In a rugby conversion from the sideline, the player has to kick a stationary ball with a lot of force. The diagram below explains the horizontal velocity of the ball.

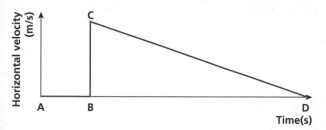

The horizontal velocity of a rugby ball

Using Newton's first and second laws of motion, explain the changes in horizontal velocity that occur in the ball from A to B (before the kick), B to C (during the kick) and C to D (following the kick).

When the ball is in flight, which factors will affect the horizontal distance of the kick? Sketch a diagram to show how you would represent the resultant force acting on the rugby ball in flight.

[20 marks]

This extended synoptic question requires knowledge from different topic areas within biomechanics. You need to relate Newton's laws of motion to the graph of the kick and demonstrate knowledge of the factors that affect how far the kick goes. Finally, you need to draw a parallelogram of the forces acting on the kick.

Student A

At A to B the ball is stationary AO2 because there is no horizontal velocity AO1. At B, Newton's first law of inertia has been demonstrated AO2, because the horizontal velocity of the ball has changed AO2. This law states that 'every body continues in its state of rest or motion in a straight line, unless compelled to change that state by external forces exerted upon it' AO1. In terms of the kick, the ball will remain on the kicking cone in a state of rest until the rugby player exerts a muscular force upon it AO2 using their quadriceps as they extend the knee AO2. Also, the ball will continue to act as a projectile in a state of motion until it hits the ground AO2.

20/20 marks awarded This is a comprehensive level-4 answer. Knowledge of all three biomechanical areas is detailed and technical, and the specialist vocabulary is accurate. This knowledge is applied well to the kick and therefore relevant.

C to D is when the ball is travelling through the air AO2. At first (at C) the ball is travelling quickly and its velocity decreases as it travels through the air AO2. Newton's second law of acceleration states that 'the rate of momentum of a body (or the acceleration for a body of constant mass) is proportional to the force causing it and the change that takes place in the direction in which the force acts' AO1. Force = mass × acceleration ($F = ma$) AO1. When the kicker exerts a muscular force to kick the ball, the acceleration of the kick or its rate of change of momentum is proportional to the size of the force AO1. So, the greater the muscular force from the kicking leg, the faster and further the kick will go AO3.

When kicking the ball, angle of release AO1, speed of release AO1 and height of release AO1 affect the horizontal distance of a projectile. The optimum angle of release depends on the release height and landing height. When both the release height and the landing height are equal, then the optimum angle of release is 45° AO3. If the release height is below the landing height then the optimum angle of release needs to be greater than 45° AO3. When the release height is greater than the landing height, the optimum angle of release needs to be less than 45° AO3. In a conversion in rugby the kicker needs the landing height to be above the cross-bar, so the angle of release will be greater than 45° AO3.

With speed of release, the greater the release velocity of a projectile, the greater the horizontal distance travelled AO1. This means that in order for the ball to reach the rugby posts a large muscular force is needed AO2. This can be achieved by a follow-through with the kick AO3. Height of release is not as important with a rugby conversion because the ball will always be low to the ground on the kicking cone AO3.This therefore means that the kicker has to rely on the angle and speed of release AO3.

The two forces are air resistance and weight, and these originate from the same point AO1. The resultant forces make a parallelogram AO1.

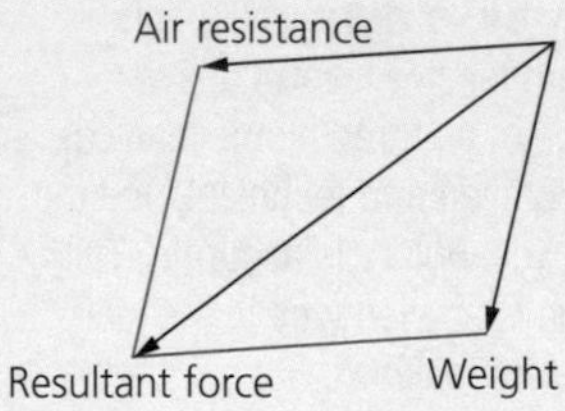

Air resistance

Resultant force   Weight

AO2

Student B

In the graph the horizontal velocity of the ball increases at B AO2 and this is because of Newton's first law, where a force is required to change the state of motion AO1. The ball's state of motion has gone from stationary to moving AO2. At C the ball is a projectile and as it moves through the air its horizontal velocity is decreasing AO2. This relates to Newton's second law of acceleration, which is force = mass × acceleration ($F = ma$) AO1.

Speed of release AO1 is important for determining the horizontal distance of the kick AO3. To achieve a greater speed, the kicker has to apply a lot of force to the ball AO2.

5/20 marks awarded This answer only achieves level 1. The knowledge that has been demonstrated is accurate and relevant, but there is too much missing, including the required sketch, which limits the A01 mark. There is some evidence of application, but analysis is minimal and the response uses only basic technical and specialist vocabulary, most of which can be obtained from the wording of the question.

Knowledge check answers

1

Joint action	Plane	Agonist	Antagonist
Hip abduction	Frontal	Gluteus medius/minimus	Adductors longus, brevis and magnus
Knee extension	Sagittal	Rectus femoris	Biceps femoris

2 Slow oxidative

3 Higher. This increases the oxygen carrying capacity of the blood to the muscles, enabling the performer to work harder for longer (more aerobic energy production).

4 Stroke volume increases, resting heart rate decreases and cardiac output stays the same. It is maximum cardiac output that increases.

5 The SA node sends impulses through the walls of the atria, causing them to contract (atrial systole).

The impulse then passes through the AV node into the bundle of His, which branches into two bundle branches and into the Purkinje fibres.

These are spread throughout the ventricles, causing them to contract (ventricular systole).

6 The increase in carbon dioxide is picked up by chemoreceptors. These send impulses to the cardiac control centre in the medulla oblongata.

Sympathetic impulses are then sent:
- to the SA node
- to increase heart rate

7 1 mark for a definition of diffusion — high concentration/partial pressure to low concentration/partial pressure/down a concentration/diffusion gradient

There is a higher pO_2 in the blood and a lower pO_2 in the muscles, so oxygen moves from the blood into the muscles.

There is a higher pCO_2 in the muscles and a lower pCO_2 in the blood, so carbon dioxide moves from the muscles into the blood.

8 (a) ATP-PC system; (b) glycolytic system; (c) aerobic system

9 Restoration of ATP and PC; resaturation of myoglobin with oxygen

10 Acclimatisation can improve altitude sickness, poor sleep and headaches.

It allows for detraining.

11 Sedentary lifestyle — need to eat less food as they do not need as much energy as a trained performer

Endurance athlete — more carbohydrates and unsaturated fats, because they need lots of energy for long-duration exercise

Power athlete — more protein for muscle growth and repair as muscles experience more strain due to the explosive nature of their sport

12 BMR + TEF + the energy expended in physical activity

13 Steroids increase muscle mass and strength, so this will increase their chance of running a faster time.

Allows them to train for longer and at a higher intensity, which would improve their times.

Allows them to recover more quickly.

However, risks involved include aggression, mood swings, liver damage, heart failure, acne and hormonal disturbances.

Steroids are also illegal, so an athlete who takes them will be cheating/which raises ethical considerations.

14 Infections such as hepatitis and HIV

Increased blood viscosity

Decreased cardiac output

Increased risk of blood clots and heart disease

Risk of transfusion

Ethical considerations — blood doping is cheating/illegal and can lead to a sporting ban

15 Decreases due to a decrease in plasma volume and stroke volume and an increased temperature and heart rate.

16 Gradually increase the number of sessions completed per week/or equivalent example

Increase number of work periods in a set/number of sets

Decrease number of rest periods

17 Macro-, meso- and microcycles

18 Fartlek training improves aerobic capacity (VO_2 max), which is important for a games player as they predominantly work aerobically during the game. A football game, for example, lasts 90 minutes. However, there are times during a game where intensity is high, and this is the same in fartlek training, where intensity is varied. This makes fartlek training more game specific.

19 Increases stroke volume and lowers resting heart rate

20 An endurance performer will do lighter weights and with more repetitions and sets, while a power athlete will lift much heavier weights with fewer repetitions and sets.

21 Any three from:
- Increases ATP, PC and glycogen stores in the muscle
- Enzyme activity increases
- Increase in the buffering capacity of the blood, which delays OBLA
- Increase in muscle mass helps to manage body weight through greater energy expenditure.

22 A gymnast requires a lot of flexibility, so needs to use a method of flexibility training that can push the joints even further, such as ballistic stretching or PNF.

23 Acute — any injury caused suddenly, for example a muscle strain or bone fracture

Chronic — any overuse injury, for example tendonitis or shin splints

24 An intrinsic risk factor is an injury risk or force from inside the body. An extrinsic risk factor is an injury risk or force from outside the body.

25 Any example of a soft tissue injury, for example muscle strain or ligament sprain

26 Cold therapy reduces the temperature of an injury and has an analgesic effect because it reduces swelling, bleeding and pain.

27 Any two from:
- Friction allows the sprinter to travel forward through grip from their spikes.
- Air resistance opposes motion.
- Weight acts in a downwards direction from their centre of mass.
- A reaction force acts vertically upwards from the foot, where it contacts the ground.

28 Lower the centre of mass
Keep the line of gravity central over the base of support

The more contact points, the larger the base of support becomes, for example keep two feet on the ground wherever possible.

29 Second-class lever, which can move a large load over a short distance and requires little effort

30 When moment of inertia is high, angular velocity is low (and vice versa).

31 By increasing his moment of inertia the diver reduces his angular velocity, which reduces the rate of spin, so he will be able to control his entry into the water.

32 Speed of release, angle of release and height of release

33 The angle of attack changes the flow of air around the javelin, so the air that travels under the javelin has to travel a shorter distance than the air above. This results in the air below the javelin travelling at a slower velocity, which therefore creates a higher pressure. This higher pressure creates an upward lift force and allows the javelin to travel further.

Index